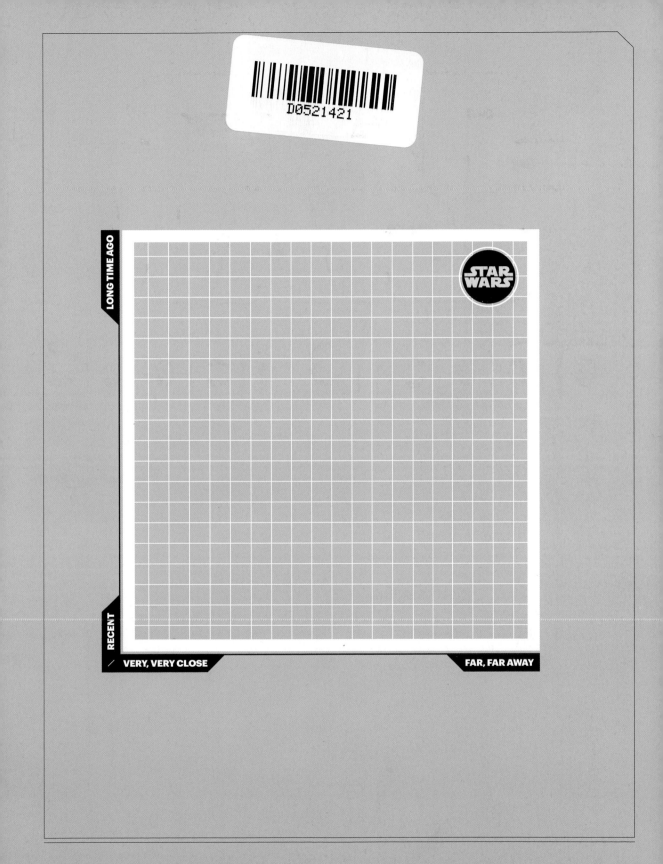

LONG TIME AGO

RECENT

/ VERY, VERY CLOSE

FAR, FAR AWAY

STAR WARS

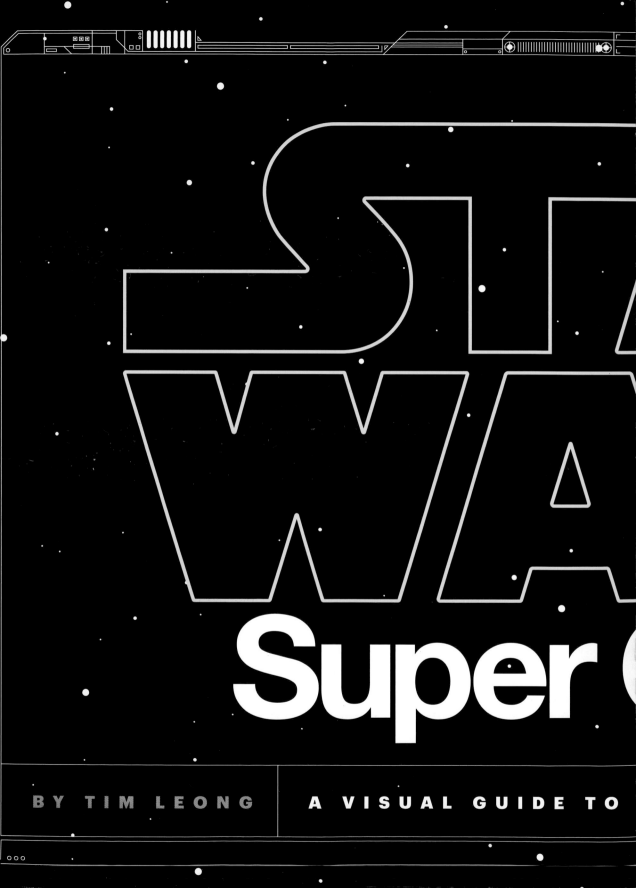

STAR WARS

Super G

BY TIM LEONG

A VISUAL GUIDE TO

STAR WARS

™

Graphic

A GALAXY FAR, FAR AWAY

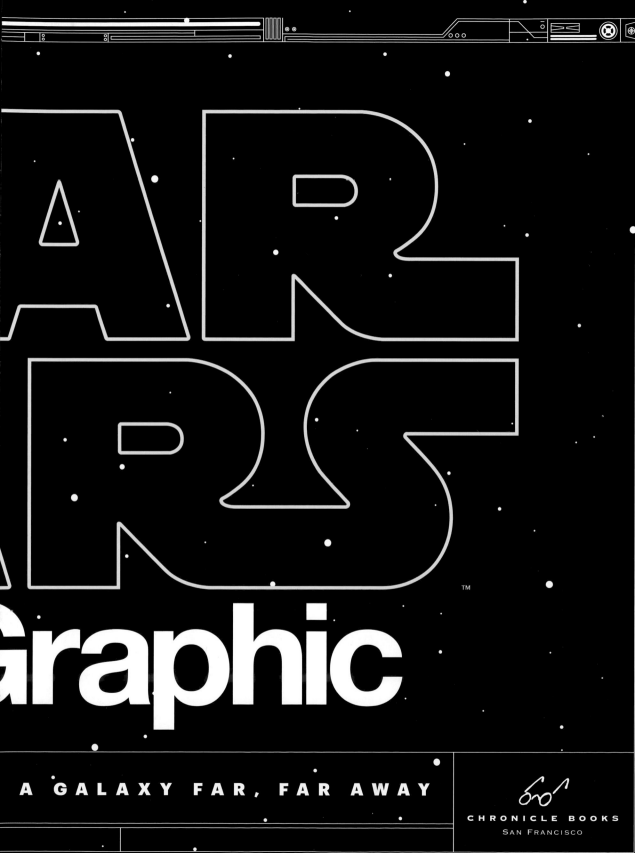

CHRONICLE BOOKS
SAN FRANCISCO

EVERYTHING YOU NEVER WANTED TO

NUMBER OF WORDS IN EACH OPENING CRAWL

STAR WARS: EPISODE I *THE PHANTOM MENACE*

STAR WARS: EPISODE II *ATTACK OF THE CLONES*

STAR WARS: EPISODE III *REVENGE OF THE SITH*

STAR WARS: EPISODE IV *A NEW HOPE*

STAR WARS: EPISODE V *THE EMPIRE STRIKES BACK*

STAR WARS: EPISODE VI *RETURN OF THE JEDI*

STAR WARS: EPISODE VII *THE FORCE AWAKENS*

TO HIGHLIGHT THE FILM'S PLOT AND THEMES, THESE WORDS WERE IN ALL-CAPS →

THE DIRECTION THE CAMERA PANS AFTER THE OPENING CREDITS

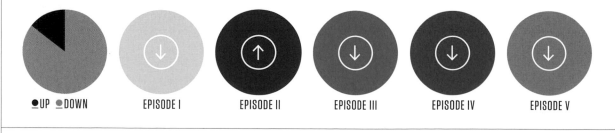

●UP ●DOWN   EPISODE I   EPISODE II   EPISODE III   EPISODE IV   EPISODE V

FONTS   THERE ARE TWO TYPEFACES USED IN THE OPENING CREDITS: **NEWS GOTHIC BOLD** FOR THE MAIN TEXT AND

KNOW ABOUT THE OPENING CRAWL

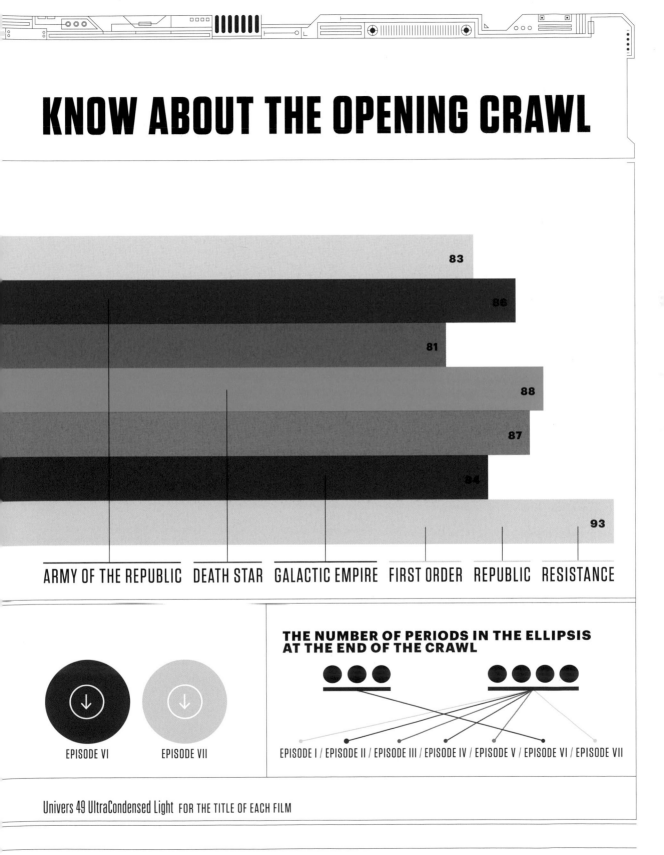

83

86

81

88

87

84

93

ARMY OF THE REPUBLIC   DEATH STAR   GALACTIC EMPIRE   FIRST ORDER   REPUBLIC   RESISTANCE

EPISODE VI   EPISODE VII

THE NUMBER OF PERIODS IN THE ELLIPSIS AT THE END OF THE CRAWL

EPISODE I / EPISODE II / EPISODE III / EPISODE IV / EPISODE V / EPISODE VI / EPISODE VII

Univers 49 UltraCondensed Light FOR THE TITLE OF EACH FILM

WHERE IN THE WORLD IS

	THE PHANTOM MENACE	ATTACK OF THE CLONES	STAR WARS: THE CLONE WARS	REVENGE OF THE SITH
ADMIRAL ACKBAR			●	
AHSOKA TANO			●	
ANAKIN SKYWALKER	●	●	●	●
BOBA FETT		●	●	
C-3PO	●	●	●	●
CHEWBACCA			●	●
COUNT DOOKU		●	●	●
DARTH VADER			VISION	●
SHEEV PALPATINE	●	●	●	●
GENERAL GRIEVOUS			●	●
HAN SOLO				
JABBA THE HUTT	●		●	
LEIA ORGANA				●
LUKE SKYWALKER				●
MACE WINDU	●	●	●	●
MON MOTHMA			●	●
OBI-WAN KENOBI	●	●	●	●
PADMÉ AMIDALA	●	●	●	●
QUI-GON JINN	●		●	MENTIONED
R2-D2	●	●	●	●
WILHUFF TARKIN			●	●
YODA	●	●	●	●

BOBA FETT?

Which characters appear in which adventure.

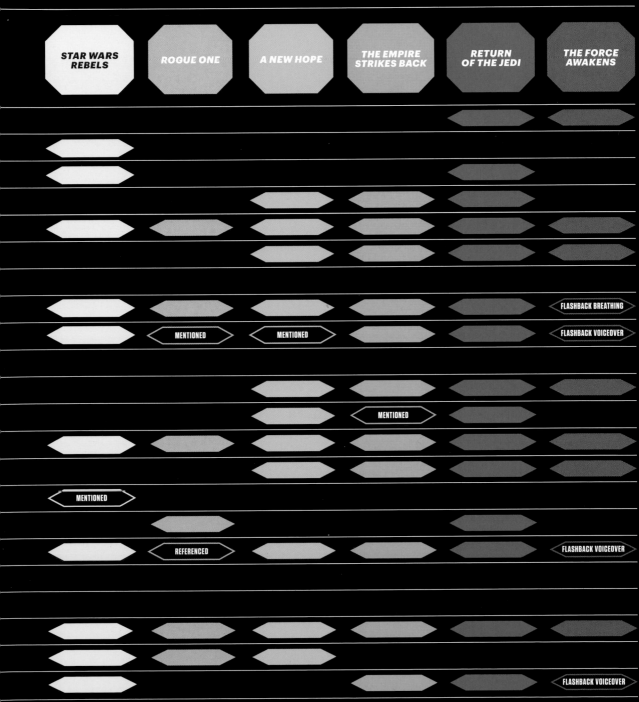

STAR WARS REBELS	ROGUE ONE	A NEW HOPE	THE EMPIRE STRIKES BACK	RETURN OF THE JEDI	THE FORCE AWAKENS
				●	●
●					
●				●	
		●	●	●	
●	●	●	●	●	●
		●	●		
●	●	●	●	●	FLASHBACK BREATHING
●	MENTIONED	MENTIONED	●	●	FLASHBACK VOICEOVER
		●	●	●	●
		●	MENTIONED		
●	●	●	●	●	●
		●	●	●	●
MENTIONED					
	●			●	
●	REFERENCED	●	●	●	FLASHBACK VOICEOVER
●	●	●	●	●	●
●	●	●			
●			●	●	FLASHBACK VOICEOVER

WAIT, WHERE DO I START?

START

- STAR WARS: DARTH MAUL
- STAR WARS: EPISODE I THE PHANTOM MENACE
- STAR WARS: OBI-WAN & ANAKIN
- STAR WARS: EPISODE II ATTACK OF THE CLONES
- STAR WARS: THE CLONE WARS
- STAR WARS: THE CLONE WARS
- STAR WARS: DARTH MAUL—SON OF DATHOMIR
- DARK DISCIPLE
- STAR WARS: KANAN
- STAR WARS: EPISODE III REVENGE OF THE SITH
- AHSOKA
- ADVENTURES IN WILD SPACE
- LORDS OF THE SITH
- TARKIN
- A NEW DAWN
- STAR WARS REBELS
- LOST STARS
- CATALYST
- ROGUE ONE: A STAR WARS STORY
- STAR WARS: EPISODE IV A NEW HOPE
- SMUGGLER'S RUN
- WEAPON OF A JEDI
- STAR WARS: PRINCESS LEIA

Continuing the stories outside of the movies has always been part of the *Star Wars* tradition, through books, comics, video games, and more. With new movies on the horizon ready to expand the canon—the immovable mythos—of the saga, Lucasfilm took the opportunity to align its storytelling with the rich possibilities of stories yet to be told. The published works going forward from 2014, unless otherwise noted, would be part of this canon. This book uses only this material, and this chart puts this reading list into a suggested order.

● MOVIE
○ TV
● NOVEL
○ COMIC BOOK

FINISH

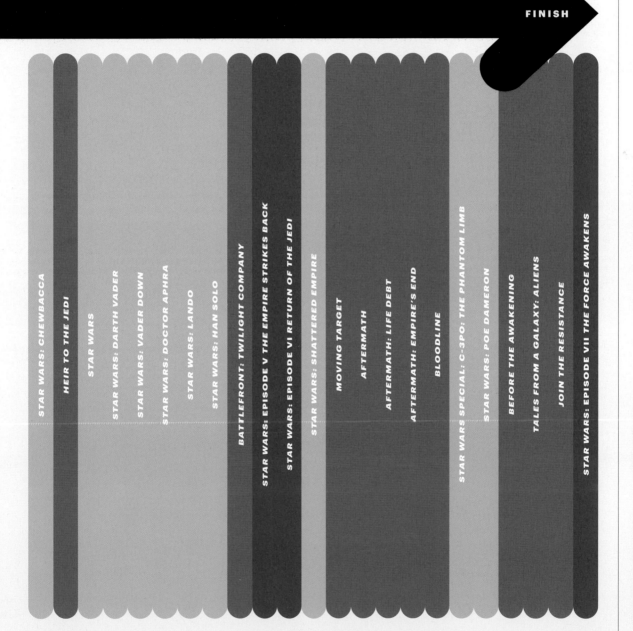

STAR WARS: CHEWBACCA

HEIR TO THE JEDI

STAR WARS

STAR WARS: DARTH VADER

STAR WARS: VADER DOWN

STAR WARS: DOCTOR APHRA

STAR WARS: LANDO

STAR WARS: HAN SOLO

BATTLEFRONT: TWILIGHT COMPANY

STAR WARS: EPISODE V THE EMPIRE STRIKES BACK

STAR WARS: EPISODE VI RETURN OF THE JEDI

STAR WARS: SHATTERED EMPIRE

MOVING TARGET

AFTERMATH

AFTERMATH: LIFE DEBT

AFTERMATH: EMPIRE'S END

BLOODLINE

STAR WARS SPECIAL: C-3PO: THE PHANTOM LIMB

STAR WARS: POE DAMERON

BEFORE THE AWAKENING

TALES FROM A GALAXY: ALIENS

JOIN THE RESISTANCE

STAR WARS: EPISODE VII THE FORCE AWAKENS

A GALAXY FAR, FAR AWAY

An intergalactic map to the *Stars*.

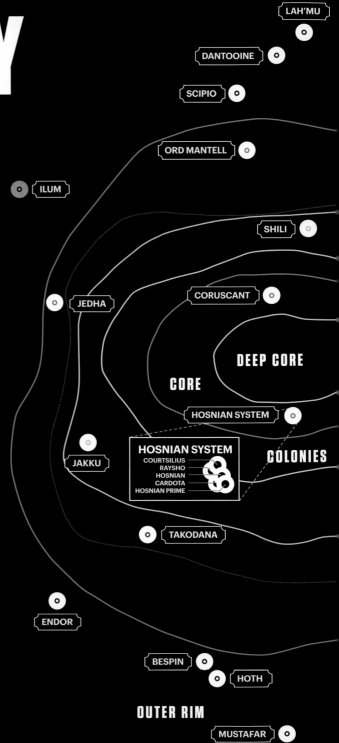

ENDOR

Its forest moon of the same name was home to the Ewoks and also the shield generator for the Death Star II.

JAKKU

The final battle between the Empire and the rebels was here. Rey is from here.

JEDHA

Once a place of holy pilgrimage, Saw Gerrera has a hideout here during Imperial occupation.

BESPIN

Lando Calrissian's Cloud City sat above this giant gas-producing planet.

HOTH

The rebels used this remote ice planet for Echo Base, their headquarters in *The Empire Strikes Back*.

TAKODANA

A haven for smugglers and outlaws, it was a perfect setting for Maz Kanata's castle.

ILUM

Every Jedi goes to this ice planet to find a kyber crystal—the power source of their lightsaber.

CORUSCANT

The entire planet is covered by the city, and was home to the galactic capital.

SHILI

Togrutas like Ahsoka Tano and Shaak Ti hail from this grassland planet.

MUSTAFAR

Obi-Wan Kenobi dueled Anakin Skywalker on this lava planet, slicing off his apprentice's limbs in the process.

ALDERAAN

Grand Moff Tarkin destroys Leia Organa's home planet (with Bail Organa on it) with the Death Star.

CORELLIA

Han Solo was born here, and the *Millennium Falcon* was built here.

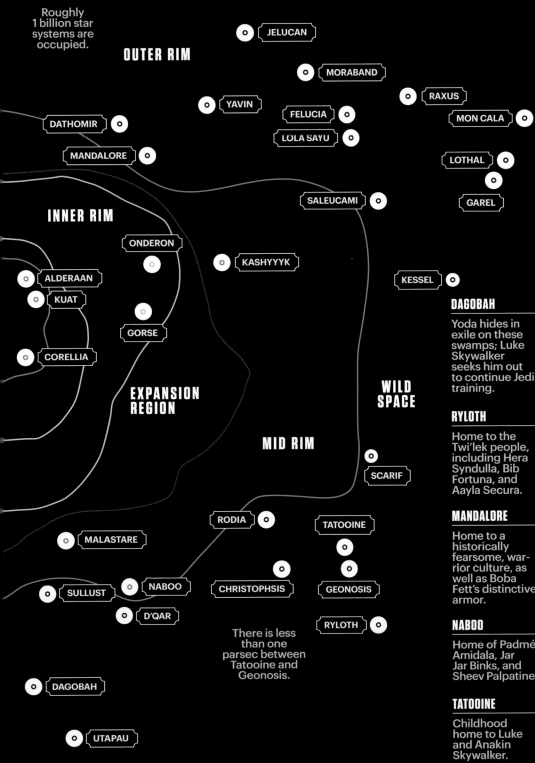

Roughly 1 billion star systems are occupied.

OUTER RIM

INNER RIM

EXPANSION REGION

MID RIM

WILD SPACE

JELUCAN

MORABAND

YAVIN

DATHOMIR

FELUCIA

LOLA SAYU

MANDALORE

RAXUS

MON CALA

LOTHAL

GAREL

SALEUCAMI

ONDERON

KASHYYYK

KESSEL

ALDERAAN

KUAT

GORSE

CORELLIA

RODIA

TATOOINE

MALASTARE

SCARIF

CHRISTOPHSIS

GEONOSIS

NABOO

SULLUST

D'QAR

RYLOTH

There is less than one parsec between Tatooine and Geonosis.

DAGOBAH

UTAPAU

JELUCAN

Home of Thane Kyrell and Ciena Ree.

YAVIN

The rebels destroyed the first Death Star near this planet's moon (and rebel base), Yavin 4.

GEONOSIS

Obi-Wan is captured while investigating a droid factory— the fight for his rescue is the first battle of the Clone Wars.

DATHOMIR

Home to Mother Talzin's Nightsisters, as well as their Nightbrothers (including the Zabrak Darth Maul).

SCARIF

The main construction outpost for the Imperial war machine.

LOTHAL

The rebel cell featuring Ezra Bridger formed here on his home planet.

KASHYYYK

The tree-covered home world to the Wookiees.

KAMINO

Purged from the Jedi archives, this hidden ocean world mass-produces clones.

DAGOBAH

Yoda hides in exile on these swamps; Luke Skywalker seeks him out to continue Jedi training.

RYLOTH

Home to the Twi'lek people, including Hera Syndulla, Bib Fortuna, and Aayla Secura.

MANDALORE

Home to a historically fearsome, warrior culture, as well as Boba Fett's distinctive armor.

NABOO

Home of Padmé Amidala, Jar Jar Binks, and Sheev Palpatine.

TATOOINE

Childhood home to Luke and Anakin Skywalker.

Ilum
DIAMETER
660 KM

DAYS IN THE YEAR
301

SIGNIFICANCE
KYBER CRYSTALS
GROW HERE

Mustafar
DIAMETER
4,200 KM

DAYS IN THE YEAR
412

SIGNIFICANCE
WHERE ANAKIN
FOUGHT OBI-WAN

Endor
DIAMETER
4,900 KM

DAYS IN THE YEAR
402

SIGNIFICANCE
HOME OF THE
EWOKS

Hoth
DIAMETER
7,200 KM

DAYS IN THE YEAR
549

SIGNIFICANCE
EPISODE V
STARTS HERE

Mandalore
DIAMETER
9,200 KM

DAYS IN THE YEAR
366

SIGNIFICANCE
HOME OF BOBA
FETT'S ARMOR

← SIZE OF THE DEATH STAR: 160 KM

SIZE MATTERS

How key planets (and moons) stack up against one other.

LOCATION   ● CORE WORLD   ● MID RIM   ● OUTER RIM   ○ UNKNOWN REGION

Coruscant
DIAMETER
12,240 KM

DAYS IN THE YEAR
368

SIGNIFICANCE
CAPITAL OF THE
REPUBLIC

Alderaan
DIAMETER
12,500 KM

DAYS IN THE YEAR
364

SIGNIFICANCE
LEIA WAS
PRINCESS HERE

Kashyyyk
DIAMETER
12,765 KM

DAYS IN THE YEAR
381

SIGNIFICANCE
HOME OF THE
WOOKIEES

Dagobah
DIAMETER
14,410 KM

DAYS IN THE YEAR
341

SIGNIFICANCE
YODA EXILED
HIMSELF HERE

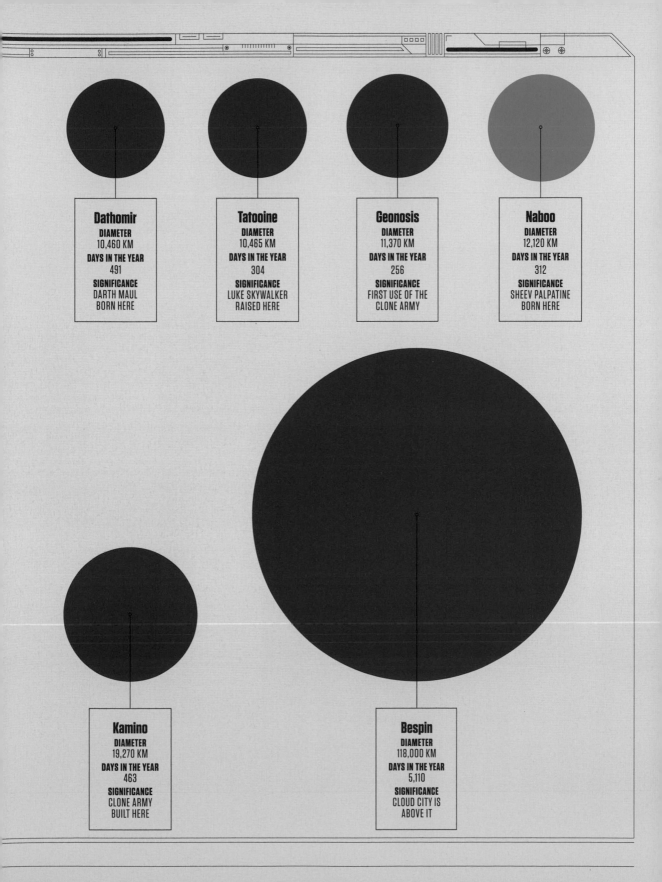

Dathomir

DIAMETER
10,460 KM

DAYS IN THE YEAR
491

SIGNIFICANCE
DARTH MAUL
BORN HERE

Tatooine

DIAMETER
10,465 KM

DAYS IN THE YEAR
304

SIGNIFICANCE
LUKE SKYWALKER
RAISED HERE

Geonosis

DIAMETER
11,370 KM

DAYS IN THE YEAR
256

SIGNIFICANCE
FIRST USE OF THE
CLONE ARMY

Naboo

DIAMETER
12,120 KM

DAYS IN THE YEAR
312

SIGNIFICANCE
SHEEV PALPATINE
BORN HERE

Kamino

DIAMETER
19,270 KM

DAYS IN THE YEAR
463

SIGNIFICANCE
CLONE ARMY
BUILT HERE

Bespin

DIAMETER
118,000 KM

DAYS IN THE YEAR
5,110

SIGNIFICANCE
CLOUD CITY IS
ABOVE IT

GALACTIC HISTORY LESSON

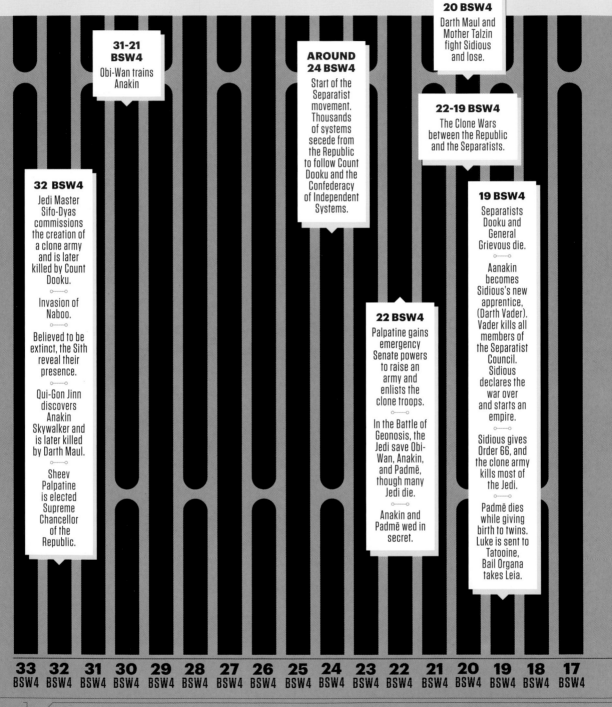

31-21 BSW4

Obi-Wan trains Anakin

AROUND 24 BSW4

Start of the Separatist movement. Thousands of systems secede from the Republic to follow Count Dooku and the Confederacy of Independent Systems.

20 BSW4

Darth Maul and Mother Talzin fight Sidious and lose.

22-19 BSW4

The Clone Wars between the Republic and the Separatists.

32 BSW4

Jedi Master Sifo-Dyas commissions the creation of a clone army and is later killed by Count Dooku.

Invasion of Naboo.

Believed to be extinct, the Sith reveal their presence.

Qui-Gon Jinn discovers Anakin Skywalker and is later killed by Darth Maul.

Sheev Palpatine is elected Supreme Chancellor of the Republic.

22 BSW4

Palpatine gains emergency Senate powers to raise an army and enlists the clone troops.

In the Battle of Geonosis, the Jedi save Obi-Wan, Anakin, and Padmē, though many Jedi die.

Anakin and Padmē wed in secret.

19 BSW4

Separatists Dooku and General Grievous die.

Aanakin becomes Sidious's new apprentice, (Darth Vader). Vader kills all members of the Separatist Council. Sidious declares the war over and starts an empire.

Sidious gives Order 66, and the clone army kills most of the Jedi.

Padmē dies while giving birth to twins. Luke is sent to Tatooine, Bail Organa takes Leia.

33 BSW4	32 BSW4	31 BSW4	30 BSW4	29 BSW4	28 BSW4	27 BSW4	26 BSW4	25 BSW4	24 BSW4	23 BSW4	22 BSW4	21 BSW4	20 BSW4	19 BSW4	18 BSW4	17 BSW4

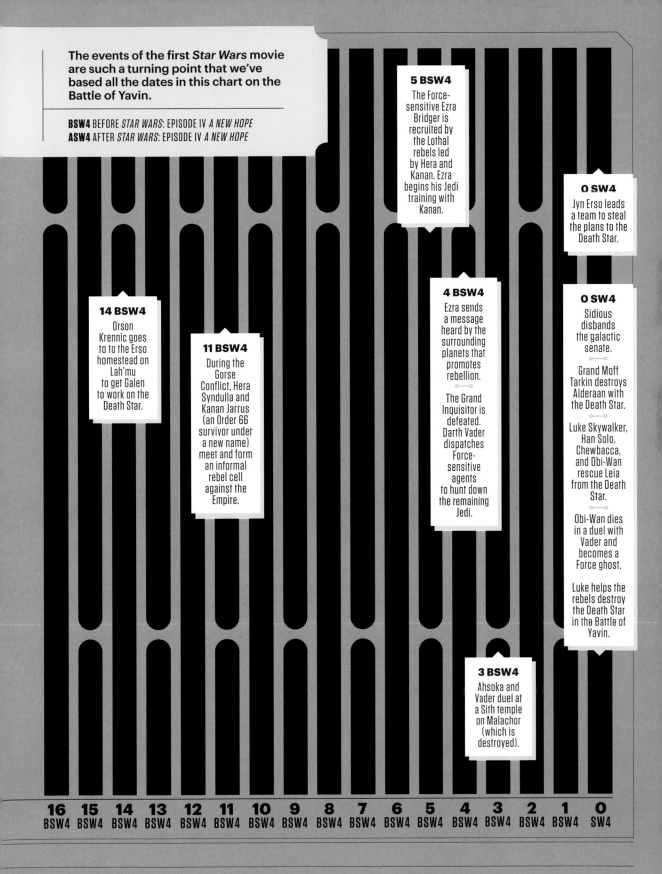

The events of the first *Star Wars* movie are such a turning point that we've based all the dates in this chart on the Battle of Yavin.

BSW4 BEFORE *STAR WARS*: EPISODE IV *A NEW HOPE*
ASW4 AFTER *STAR WARS*: EPISODE IV *A NEW HOPE*

5 BSW4
The Force-sensitive Ezra Bridger is recruited by the Lothal rebels led by Hera and Kanan. Ezra begins his Jedi training with Kanan.

0 SW4
Jyn Erso leads a team to steal the plans to the Death Star.

14 BSW4
Orson Krennic goes to to the Erso homestead on Lah'mu to get Galen to work on the Death Star.

11 BSW4
During the Gorse Conflict, Hera Syndulla and Kanan Jarrus (an Order 66 survivor under a new name) meet and form an informal rebel cell against the Empire.

4 BSW4
Ezra sends a message heard by the surrounding planets that promotes rebellion.

The Grand Inquisitor is defeated. Darth Vader dispatches Force-sensitive agents to hunt down the remaining Jedi.

0 SW4
Sidious disbands the galactic senate.

Grand Moff Tarkin destroys Alderaan with the Death Star.

Luke Skywalker, Han Solo, Chewbacca, and Obi-Wan rescue Leia from the Death Star.

Obi-Wan dies in a duel with Vader and becomes a Force ghost.

Luke helps the rebels destroy the Death Star in the Battle of Yavin.

3 BSW4
Ahsoka and Vader duel at a Sith temple on Malachor (which is destroyed).

| 16 BSW4 | 15 BSW4 | 14 BSW4 | 13 BSW4 | 12 BSW4 | 11 BSW4 | 10 BSW4 | 9 BSW4 | 8 BSW4 | 7 BSW4 | 6 BSW4 | 5 BSW4 | 4 BSW4 | 3 BSW4 | 2 BSW4 | 1 BSW4 | 0 SW4 |

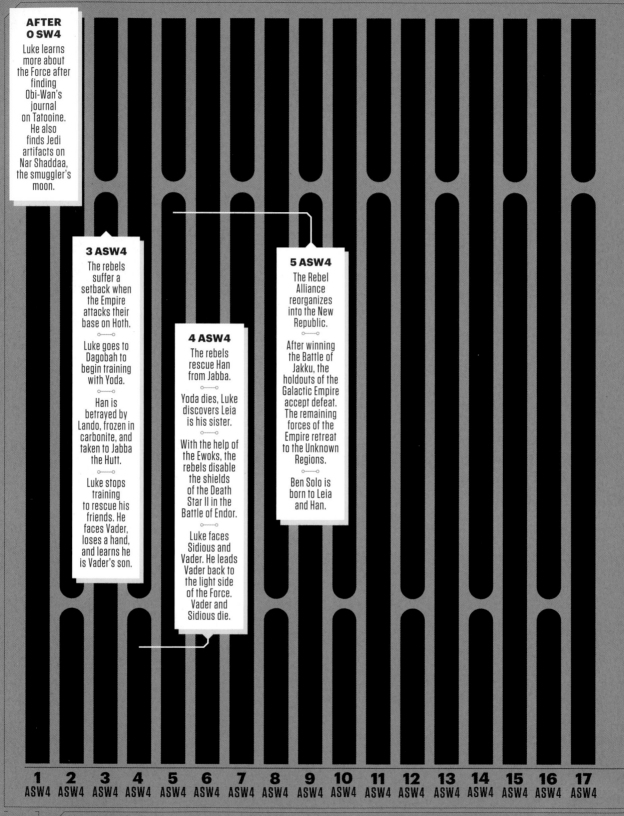

AFTER 0 SW4

Luke learns more about the Force after finding Obi-Wan's journal on Tatooine. He also finds Jedi artifacts on Nar Shaddaa, the smuggler's moon.

3 ASW4

The rebels suffer a setback when the Empire attacks their base on Hoth.

Luke goes to Dagobah to begin training with Yoda.

Han is betrayed by Lando, frozen in carbonite, and taken to Jabba the Hutt.

Luke stops training to rescue his friends. He faces Vader, loses a hand, and learns he is Vader's son.

4 ASW4

The rebels rescue Han from Jabba.

Yoda dies, Luke discovers Leia is his sister.

With the help of the Ewoks, the rebels disable the shields of the Death Star II in the Battle of Endor.

Luke faces Sidious and Vader. He leads Vader back to the light side of the Force. Vader and Sidious die.

5 ASW4

The Rebel Alliance reorganizes into the New Republic.

After winning the Battle of Jakku, the holdouts of the Galactic Empire accept defeat. The remaining forces of the Empire retreat to the Unknown Regions.

Ben Solo is born to Leia and Han.

| 1 ASW4 | 2 ASW4 | 3 ASW4 | 4 ASW4 | 5 ASW4 | 6 ASW4 | 7 ASW4 | 8 ASW4 | 9 ASW4 | 10 ASW4 | 11 ASW4 | 12 ASW4 | 13 ASW4 | 14 ASW4 | 15 ASW4 | 16 ASW4 | 17 ASW4 |

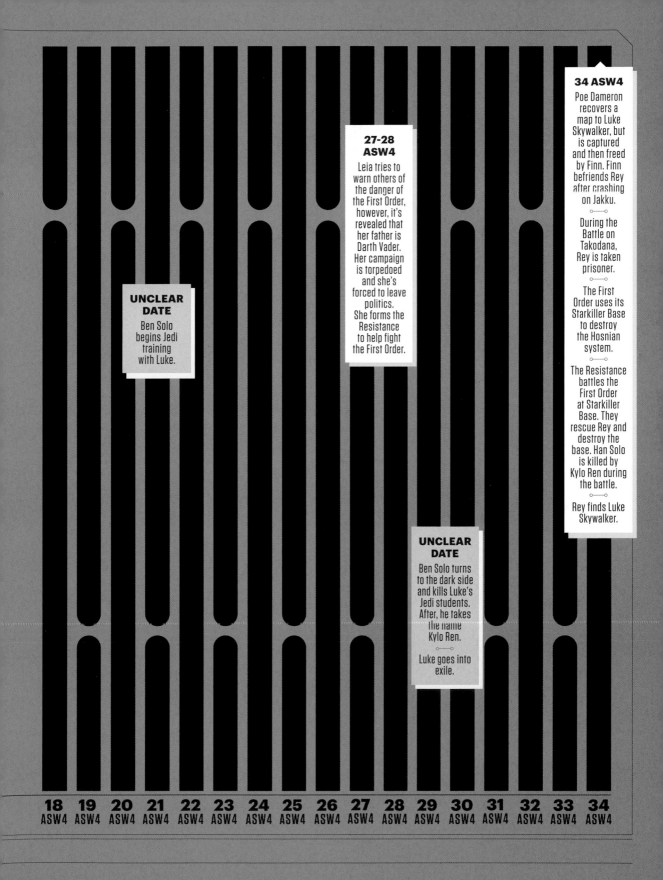

34 ASW4

Poe Dameron recovers a map to Luke Skywalker, but is captured and then freed by Finn. Finn befriends Rey after crashing on Jakku.

During the Battle on Takodana, Rey is taken prisoner.

The First Order uses its Starkiller Base to destroy the Hosnian system.

The Resistance battles the First Order at Starkiller Base. They rescue Rey and destroy the base. Han Solo is killed by Kylo Ren during the battle.

Rey finds Luke Skywalker.

27-28 ASW4

Leia tries to warn others of the danger of the First Order, however, it's revealed that her father is Darth Vader. Her campaign is torpedoed and she's forced to leave politics. She forms the Resistance to help fight the First Order.

UNCLEAR DATE

Ben Solo begins Jedi training with Luke.

UNCLEAR DATE

Ben Solo turns to the dark side and kills Luke's Jedi students. After, he takes the name Kylo Ren.

Luke goes into exile.

| 18 ASW4 | 19 ASW4 | 20 ASW4 | 21 ASW4 | 22 ASW4 | 23 ASW4 | 24 ASW4 | 25 ASW4 | 26 ASW4 | 27 ASW4 | 28 ASW4 | 29 ASW4 | 30 ASW4 | 31 ASW4 | 32 ASW4 | 33 ASW4 | 34 ASW4 |

NOT SO BAD SITUATION

"I HAVE A BAD FEELING ABOUT THIS."

—Obi-Wan Kenobi, after arriving on a Trade Federation ship

"I'VE GOT A BAD FEELING ABOUT THIS."

—Anakin Skywalker, after the Geonosians release three beasts to kill him, Padmé, and Obi-Wan at the battle arena

"OH, I HAVE A BAD FEELING ABOUT THIS."

—Obi-Wan Kenobi, before crashing his ship

"I HAVE A BAD FEELING ABO..."

—K-2SO, before trying to steal the Death Star plans on Scarif

"I HAVE A VERY BAD FEELING ABOUT THIS."

—Luke Skywalker, when approaching the Death Star

"I GOT A BAD FEELING ABOUT THIS."

—Han Solo, after hearing a disturbing sound while stuck inside a garbage masher

"I HAVE A BAD FEELING ABOUT THIS."

—Princess Leia, before realizing they're in a giant space slug and not an asteroid cavern

"ARTOO, I HAVE A BAD FEELING ABOUT THIS."

—C-3PO, while entering Jabba the Hutt's lair

"I HAVE A REALLY BAD FEELING ABOUT THIS."

—Han Solo, while being prepared to be cooked alive by the Ewoks

"I HAVE A BAD FEELING ABOUT THIS."

—Han Solo, after realizing the rathtars are loose

Star Wars: Episode I *The Phantom Menace*

Star Wars: Episode II *Attack of the Clones*

Star Wars: Episode III *Revenge of the Sith*

Rogue One: A Star Wars Story

Star Wars: Episode IV *A New Hope*

Star Wars: Episode IV *A New Hope*

Star Wars: Episode V *The Empire Strikes Back*

Star Wars: Episode VI *Return of the Jedi*

Star Wars: Episode VI *Return of the Jedi*

Star Wars: Episode VII *The Force Awakens*

LOOK WHO'S TALKING

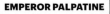

OBI-WAN KENOBI

EMPEROR PALPATINE

ANAKIN SKYWALKER/DARTH VADER

PADMÉ AMIDALA

EPISODE I

EPISODE II

EPISODE III

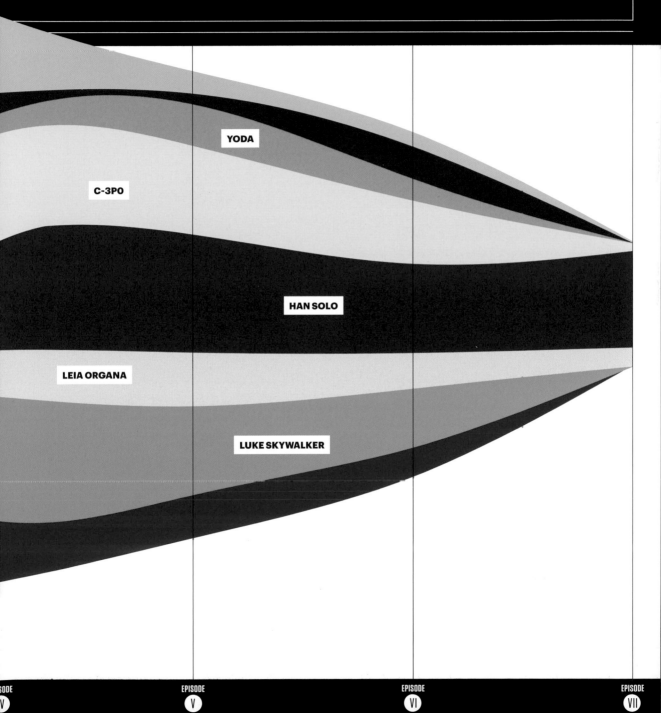

A tally of who dominated the conversation in each of the seven film episodes. Note: this tracks only major charactors who appeared in at least three films—and English speakers only (Sorry, R2!).

YODA

C-3PO

HAN SOLO

LEIA ORGANA

LUKE SKYWALKER

LUKE'S QUESTIONS, MARKED

● EPISODE IV ● EPISODE VI ● EPISODE V ● EPISODE VII		WHAT ABOUT THAT ONE?	YOU KNOW OF THE REBELLION AGAINST THE EMPIRE?	HAVE YOU BEEN IN MANY BATTLES?	WERE YOU ON A STAR CRUISER?	
HE KNEW MY FATHER?	WHAT ARE YOU DOING HIDING BACK THERE?	WHERE DO YOU THINK YOU'RE GOING?	WHAT'S WRONG WITH HIM NOW?	BEN?	BEN KENOBI?	
HOW DID MY FATHER DIE?	THE FORCE?	ALDERAAN?	HOW AM I EVER GOING TO EXPLAIN THIS?	WHY WOULD IMPERIAL TROOPS WANT TO SLAUGHTER JAWAS?	UNCLE OWEN?	
WHY DON'T YOU OUTRUN THEM?	WHAT'S THAT FLASHING?	ARE YOU ALRIGHT?	YOU MEAN IT CONTROLS YOUR ACTIONS?	YOU DON'T BELIEVE IN THE FORCE, DO YOU?	HOW AM I SUPPOSED TO FIGHT?	
WHAT DO YOU THINK...?	WHAT IS IT?	WHO?	WHO HAS HE FOUND?	THE PRINCESS?	SHE'S HERE?	
DID YOU SEE THAT?	THREEPIO?	THREEPIO?	WHERE COULD HE BE?	THREEPIO?	WHERE COULD HE BE?	
WHAT GOOD WILL IT DO US IF HE GETS HIMSELF KILLED?	IS THE SHIP ALRIGHT?	BEN?	WHAT DO YOU THINK OF HER, HAN?	SO...YOU GOT YOUR REWARD AND YOU'RE JUST LEAVING THEN?	WHY DON'T YOU TAKE A LOOK AROUND?	
BEN?	DAGOBAH SYSTEM?	CHEWIE, TAKE CARE OF YOURSELF, OKAY?	HOW ABOUT YOU?	HOBBIE, YOU STILL WITH ME?	DACK?	
ARTOO, WHAT ARE WE DOING HERE?	READY FOR SOME POWER?	NOW WILL YOU MOVE ALONG, LITTLE FELLA?	YOU KNOW HIM?	HOW FAR AWAY IS YODA?	WILL IT TAKE US LONG TO GET THERE?	
AND SACRIFICE HAN AND LEIA?	BEN, WHY DIDN'T YOU TELL ME?	BEN, WHY DIDN'T YOU TELL ME?	MASTER YODA... IS DARTH VADER MY FATHER?	UNFORTUNATE THAT I KNOW THE TRUTH?	WHY DIDN'T YOU TELL ME?	

Over the course of the films, Luke rises from naive farmboy to confident Jedi. As his confidence grows, he asks fewer and fewer questions.

WHAT'S THIS?	WHO IS SHE?	IS THERE ANY MORE TO THIS RECORDING?	WAIT A MINUTE, WHERE'D SHE GO?	DO YOU KNOW WHO HE'S TALKING ABOUT?	WHAT IF THIS OBI-WAN COMES LOOKING FOR HIM?
IS HE A RELATIVE OF YOURS?	DO YOU KNOW WHO HE'S TALKING ABOUT?	YOU KNOW HIM?	WHAT KIND OF TALK IS THAT?	YOU FOUGHT IN THE CLONE WARS?	WHAT IS IT?
AUNT BERU?	UNCLE OWEN?	DO YOU REALLY THINK WE'RE GOING TO FIND A PILOT HERE THAT'LL TAKE US TO ALDERAAN?	WHAT?	CAN I HAVE ONE OF THOSE?	TEN THOUSAND?
WHAT'S GOING ON?	WHAT DO YOU MEAN?	WHERE IS IT?	WHAT?	HOW?	WHY ARE WE STILL MOVING TOWARDS IT?
NOW ALL YOU WANT TO DO IS STAY?	THREEPIO, HAND ME THOSE BINDERS THERE, WILL YOU?	WHY DIDN'T YOU SAY SO BEFORE?	HUH?	ARE THERE ANY OTHER WAYS OUT OF THE CELL BAY?	WHAT WAS THAT?
THREEPIO, WILL YOU COME IN?	THREEPIO, WILL YOU SHUT UP AND LISTEN TO ME?	SHUT DOWN ALL GARBAGE MASHERS ON THE DETENTION LEVEL, WILL YOU?	WHERE ARE WE?	C-3PO, DO YOU COPY?	ARE YOU SAFE?
I GUESS THAT'S WHAT YOU'RE BEST AT, ISN'T IT?	YOU OKAY, ARTOO?	BLAST IT, BIGGS, WHERE ARE YOU?	HAN, OLD BUDDY, DO YOU READ ME?	WHAT'S THE MATTER?	YOU SMELL SOMETHING?
ROGUE TWO, ARE YOU ALRIGHT?	YES, ARTOO?	ARTOO?	WHERE ARE YOU?	ARE YOU ALL RIGHT?	ANYTHING BROKEN?
HOW COULD YOU KNOW MY FATHER?	IS THE DARK SIDE STRONGER?	BUT HOW AM I TO KNOW THE GOOD SIDE FROM THE BAD?	WHAT'S IN THERE?	HAN?	FUTURE? WILL THEY DIE?
A CERTAIN POINT OF VIEW?	SHE DIDN'T COME BACK?	HAN, CAN YOU REACH MY LIGHTSABER?	DO YOU UNDERSTAND ANYTHING THEY'RE SAYING?	LEIA... DO YOU REMEMBER YOUR MOTHER? YOUR REAL MOTHER?	WHAT DO YOU REMEMBER?

HISTORY OF GOVERNMENT IN THE

BSW4 BEFORE *STAR WARS*: EPISODE IV *A NEW HOPE*
ASW4 AFTER *STAR WARS*: EPISODE IV *A NEW HOPE*

AROUND 1,000 YEARS BEOFRE *STAR WARS*

GALACTIC REPUBLIC

OLD REPUBLIC

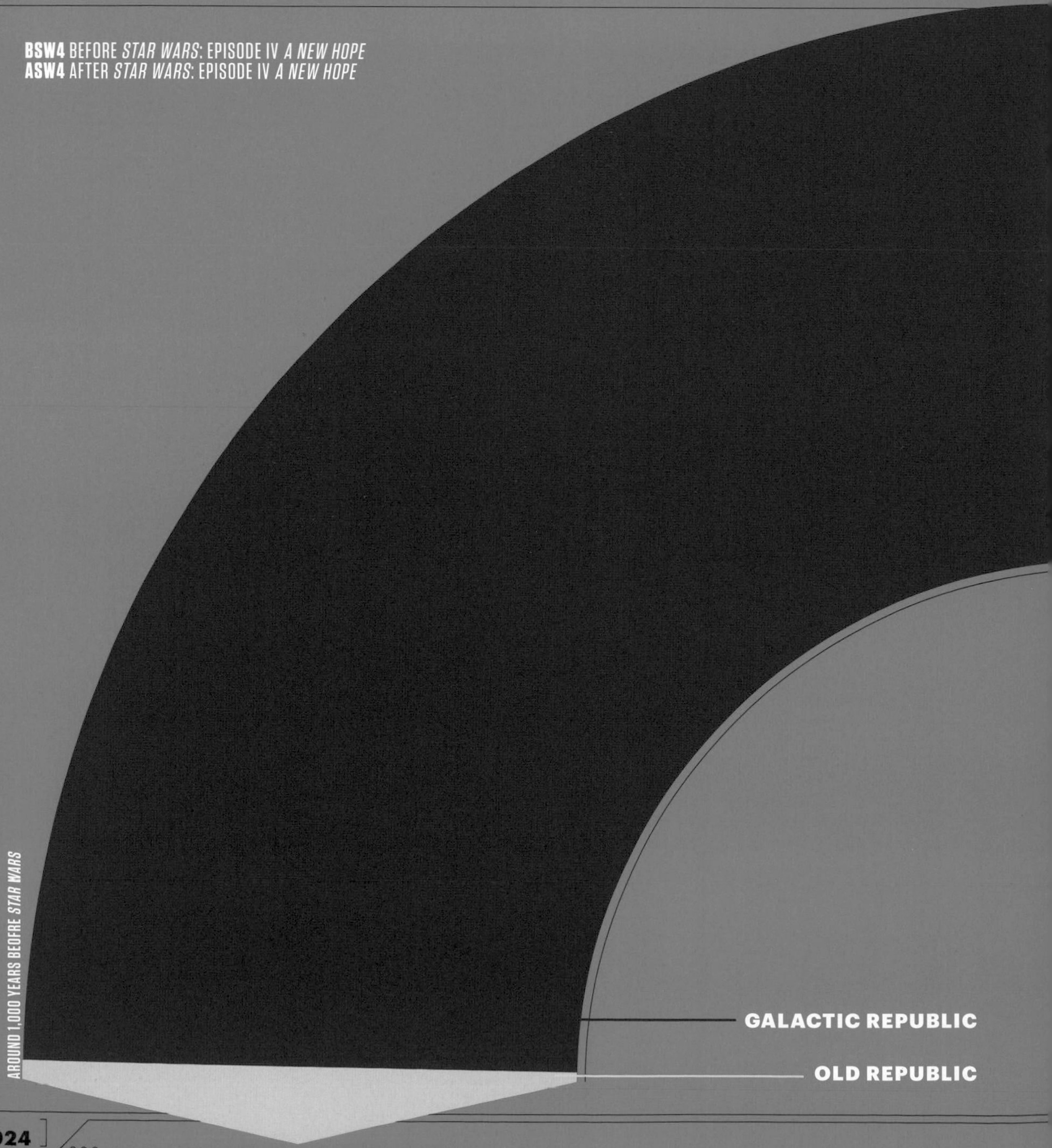

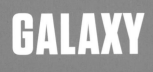

GALAXY

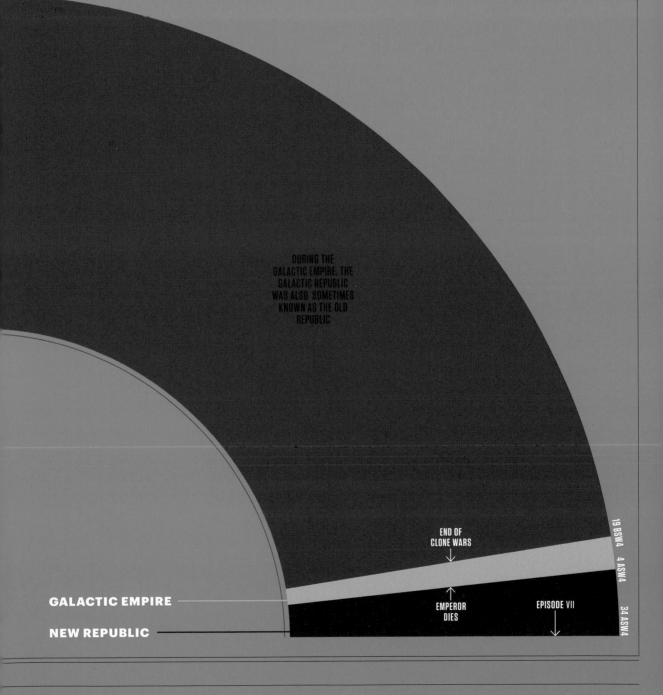

DURING THE
GALACTIC EMPIRE, THE
GALACTIC REPUBLIC
WAS ALSO SOMETIMES
KNOWN AS THE OLD
REPUBLIC

END OF
CLONE WARS
↓

EMPEROR
DIES
↑

EPISODE VII
↓

19 BSW4

4 ASW4

34 ASW4

GALACTIC EMPIRE ———————

NEW REPUBLIC ——————

"HE'S MORE MACHINE

A breakdown of how cybernetic usage, and how much person is left over.

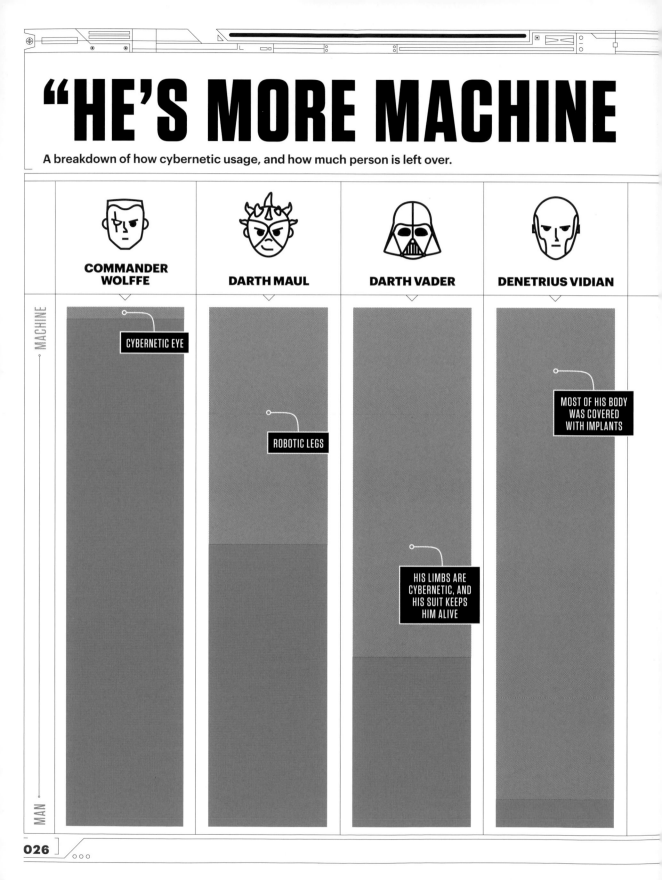

COMMANDER WOLFFE

DARTH MAUL

DARTH VADER

DENETRIUS VIDIAN

MACHINE

MAN

CYBERNETIC EYE

ROBOTIC LEGS

HIS LIMBS ARE CYBERNETIC, AND HIS SUIT KEEPS HIM ALIVE

MOST OF HIS BODY WAS COVERED WITH IMPLANTS

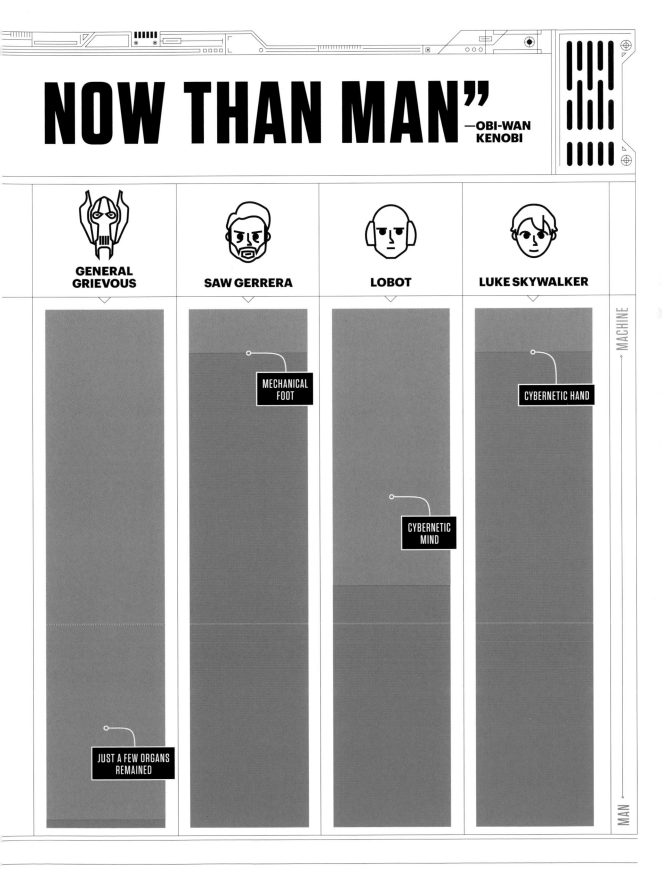

NOW THAN MAN"
—OBI-WAN KENOBI

MACHINE

GENERAL GRIEVOUS

SAW GERRERA

LOBOT

LUKE SKYWALKER

MECHANICAL FOOT

CYBERNETIC HAND

CYBERNETIC MIND

JUST A FEW ORGANS REMAINED

MAN

SHOTS FIRED

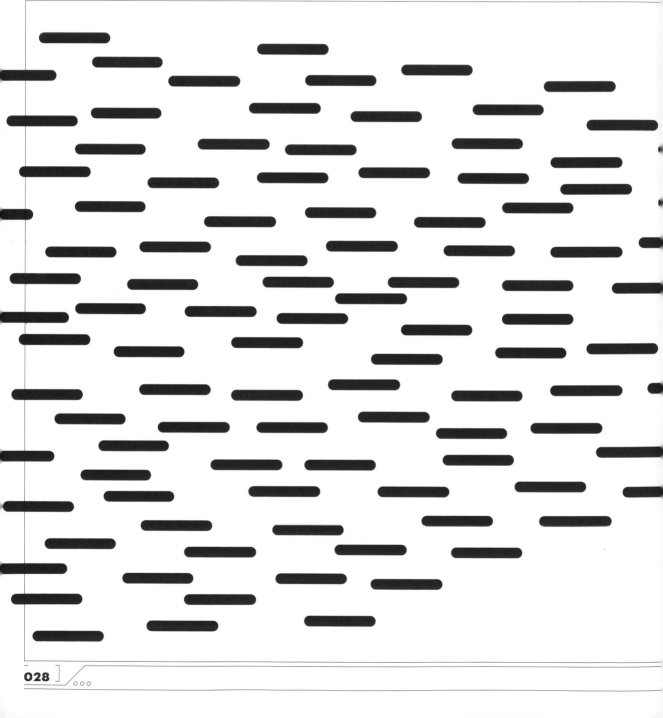

In *A New Hope*, Luke, Han, and Chewbacca attempt an improvised rescue of Princess Leia. After surviving the garbage masher, they head for the *Millennium Falcon*. They escape unscathed, but not without the Imperials taking their best shot(s).

119 MISSED BLASTER SHOTS BY STORM TROOPERS DURING THE ESCAPE.

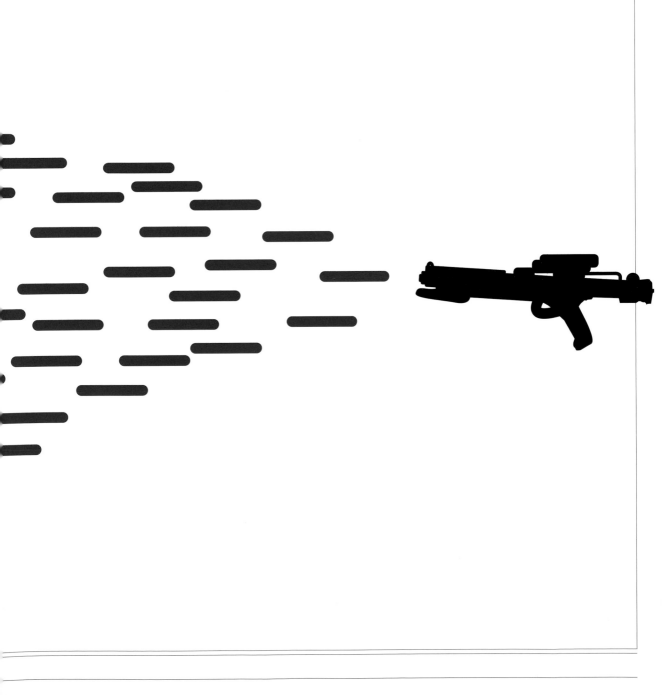

BLASTER COLORS

RED
THE MOST COMMON BLASTER COLOR, BECAUSE IT'S MADE FROM CHEAPER GAS

USED BY
STORMTROOPERS, REBELS, DROIDS, X-WINGS

GREEN
MADE FROM A HIGHER QUALITY GAS, WHICH MAKES IT MORE EXPENSIVE

USED BY
IMPERIAL STARFIGHTERS, NABOO ROYAL GUARD

BLUE
ITS ION-BASED ENERGY CHARGES ARE MORE EFFECTIVE AGAINST DROIDS AND MACHINES. A RING-SHAPED BLUE BOLT CAN ALSO SIGNIFY A STUN SETTING.

USED BY
CLONE TROOPERS IN *THE CLONE WARS*, STORMTROOPERS STUNNED LEIA IN EPISODE IV

Contrary to popuar belief, those aren't lasers that shoot out of blasters. They're energy bolts. Bolts not only vary in power, they vary in color. Here's what the shade says about the bolt.

ORANGE
THESE NON-FATAL, LOW-POWER BOLTS ARE USED IN TRAINING SITUATIONS
USED BY
LUKE'S TRAINING REMOTE, SABINE WHEN TRAINING EZRA IN *REBELS*

YELLOW
USED BY
THE MANDALORIAN TERRORIST CELL DEATH WATCH

PURPLE
USED BY
THE GEONOSIAN'S *NANTEX*-CLASS TERRITORIAL DEFENSE STARFIGHTER

LIGHT METER

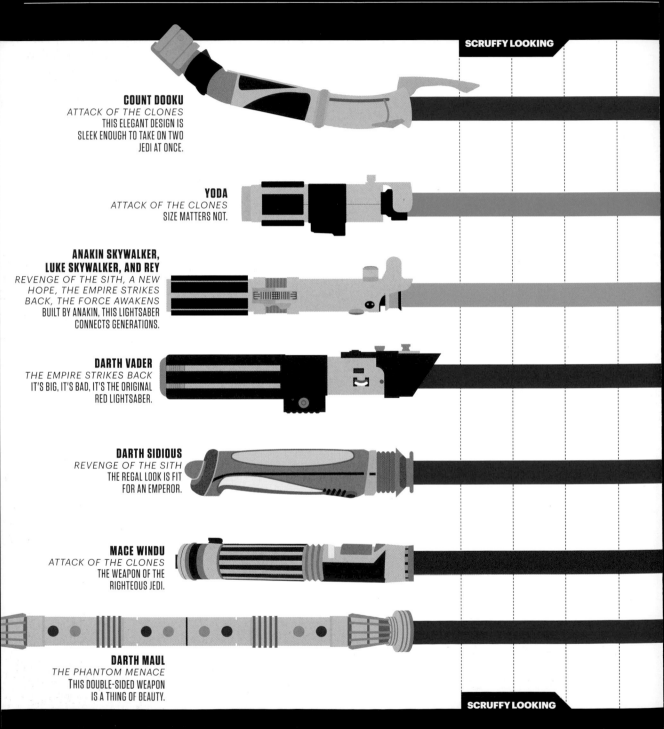

COUNT DOOKU
ATTACK OF THE CLONES
THIS ELEGANT DESIGN IS
SLEEK ENOUGH TO TAKE ON TWO
JEDI AT ONCE.

YODA
ATTACK OF THE CLONES
SIZE MATTERS NOT.

**ANAKIN SKYWALKER,
LUKE SKYWALKER, AND REY**
*REVENGE OF THE SITH, A NEW
HOPE, THE EMPIRE STRIKES
BACK, THE FORCE AWAKENS*
BUILT BY ANAKIN, THIS LIGHTSABER
CONNECTS GENERATIONS.

DARTH VADER
THE EMPIRE STRIKES BACK
IT'S BIG, IT'S BAD, IT'S THE ORIGINAL
RED LIGHTSABER.

DARTH SIDIOUS
REVENGE OF THE SITH
THE REGAL LOOK IS FIT
FOR AN EMPEROR.

MACE WINDU
ATTACK OF THE CLONES
THE WEAPON OF THE
RIGHTEOUS JEDI.

DARTH MAUL
THE PHANTOM MENACE
THIS DOUBLE-SIDED WEAPON
IS A THING OF BEAUTY.

A definitive ranking of lightsabers, based on magnificence and might.

1 OF 2

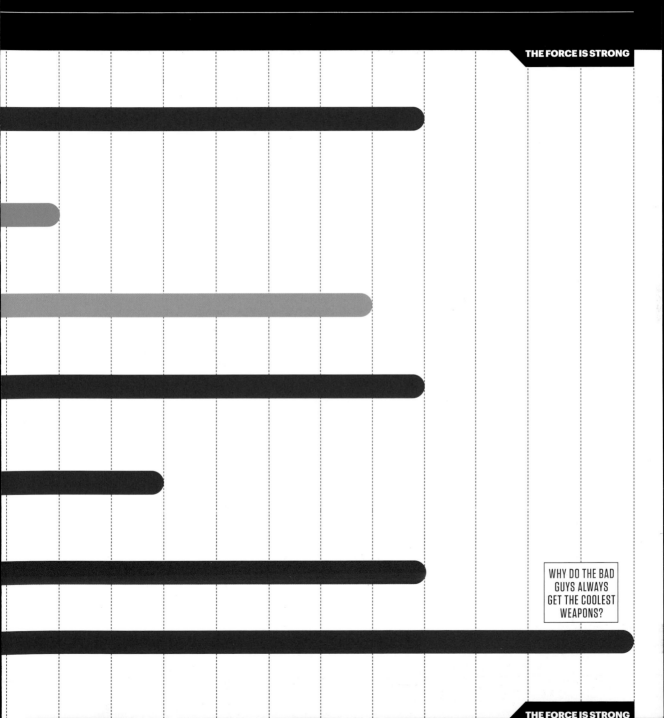

THE FORCE IS STRONG

WHY DO THE BAD GUYS ALWAYS GET THE COOLEST WEAPONS?

THE FORCE IS STRONG

LIGHT METER

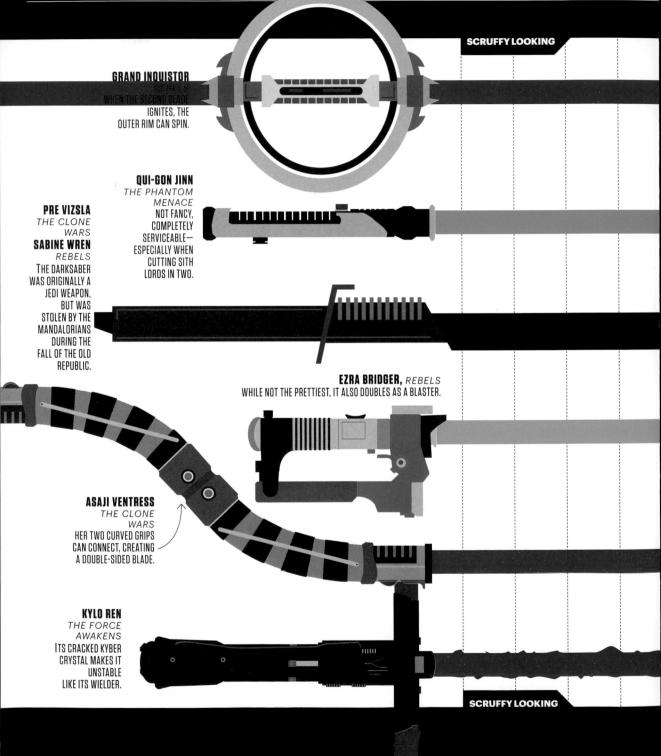

SCRUFFY LOOKING

GRAND INQUISITOR
REBELS
WHEN THE SECOND BLADE
IGNITES, THE
OUTER RIM CAN SPIN.

QUI-GON JINN
*THE PHANTOM
MENACE*
NOT FANCY,
COMPLETELY
SERVICEABLE—
ESPECIALLY WHEN
CUTTING SITH
LORDS IN TWO.

PRE VIZSLA
*THE CLONE
WARS*
SABINE WREN
REBELS
THE DARKSABER
WAS ORIGINALLY A
JEDI WEAPON,
BUT WAS
STOLEN BY THE
MANDALORIANS
DURING THE
FALL OF THE OLD
REPUBLIC.

EZRA BRIDGER, *REBELS*
WHILE NOT THE PRETTIEST, IT ALSO DOUBLES AS A BLASTER.

ASAJI VENTRESS
*THE CLONE
WARS*
HER TWO CURVED GRIPS
CAN CONNECT, CREATING
A DOUBLE-SIDED BLADE.

KYLO REN
*THE FORCE
AWAKENS*
ITS CRACKED KYBER
CRYSTAL MAKES IT
UNSTABLE
LIKE ITS WIELDER.

SCRUFFY LOOKING

A definitive ranking of lightsabers, based on magnificence and might.

2 of 2

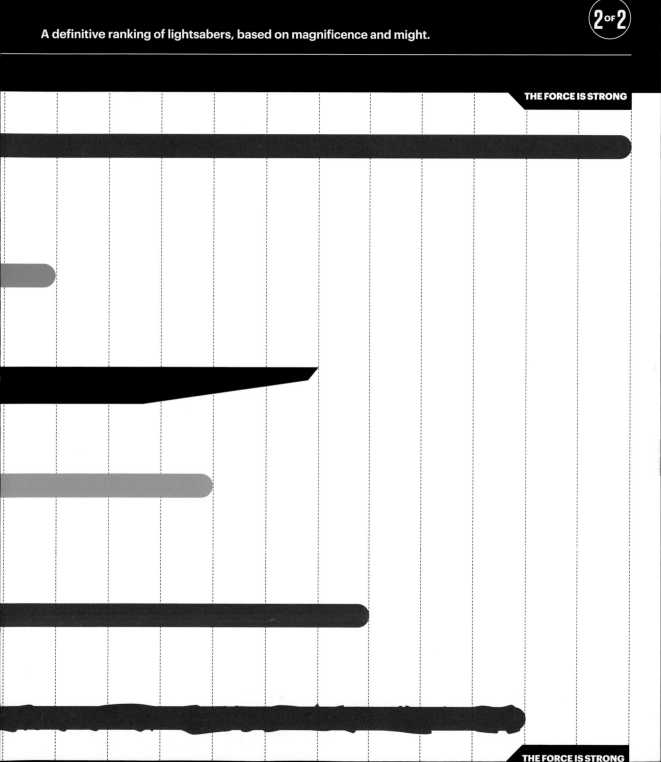

THE FORCE IS STRONG

THE LIGHTSABER LIST

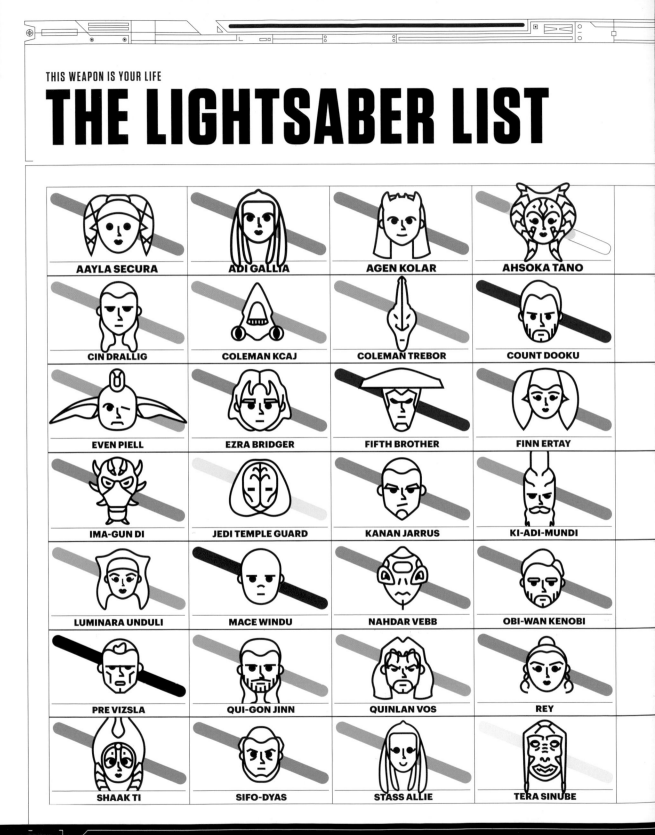

AAYLA SECURA

ADI GALLIA

AGEN KOLAR

AHSOKA TANO

CIN DRALLIG

COLEMAN KCAJ

COLEMAN TREBOR

COUNT DOOKU

EVEN PIELL

EZRA BRIDGER

FIFTH BROTHER

FINN ERTAY

IMA-GUN DI

JEDI TEMPLE GUARD

KANAN JARRUS

KI-ADI-MUNDI

LUMINARA UNDULI

MACE WINDU

NAHDAR VEBB

OBI-WAN KENOBI

PRE VIZSLA

QUI-GON JINN

QUINLAN VOS

REY

SHAAK TI

SIFO-DYAS

STASS ALLIE

TERA SINUBE

The color of a Jedi's lightsaber is based on its kyber crystal. The crystals themselves are Force-sensitive, colorless, and lead Jedi to find them. When the crystals are attuned to a Jedi they glow (typically blue or green). The only way someone from the dark side could use a kyber crystal in a lightsaber is to dominate it—causing it to "bleed" red. Which is why all Sith lightsabers are red. It is possible to "heal" the crystals—a process that turns them white (see Ahsoka Tano).

ANAKIN SKYWALKER	ASAJJ VENTRESS	BARRISS OFFEE	BULTAR SWAN
DARTH MAUL	DARTH SIDIOUS	DEPA BILLABA	EETH KOTH
GENERAL GRIEVOUS	GRAND INQUISITOR	HALSEY	HUULIK
KIT FISTO	KY NAREC	KYLO REN	LUKE SKYWALKER
OPPO RANCISIS	PABLO-JILL	PLO KOON	PONG KRELL
RIG NEMA	SAESEE TIIN	SAVAGE OPPRESS	SEVENTH SISTER
TIPLAR	TIPLEE	YARAEL POOF	YODA

STORMTROOPER COMMANDS

DARTH MAUL

- TIME SPENT AS DARTH SIDIOUS'S APPRENTICE
- TIME SPENT WITH SAVAGE OPRESS AS HIS APPRENTICE
- TIME SPENT AS THE RULER OF MANDALORE

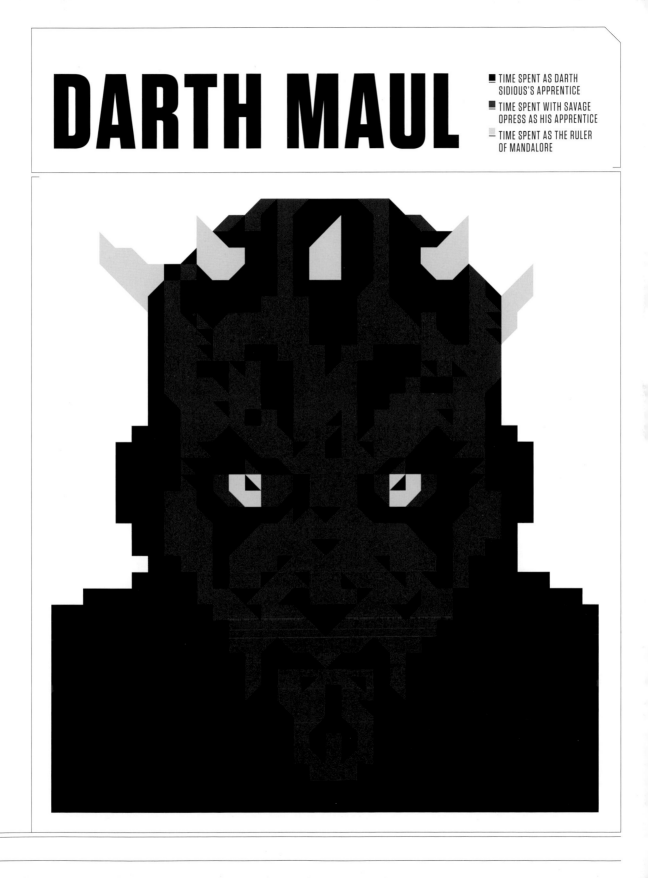

THE FORCE IS STRONG

Who name drops "Force" the most in the *Star Wars* films.

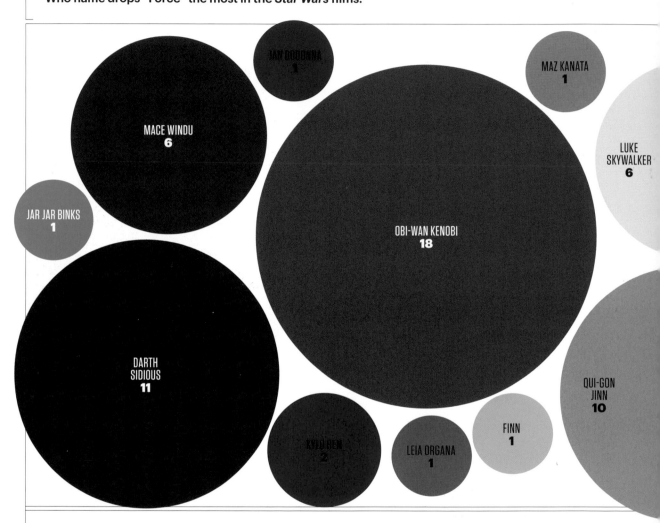

JAR JODONNA
1

MAZ KANATA
1

MACE WINDU
6

LUKE SKYWALKER
6

JAR JAR BINKS
1

OBI-WAN KENOBI
18

DARTH SIDIOUS
11

QUI-GON JINN
10

KYLO REN
2

LEIA ORGANA
1

FINN
1

NUMBER OF "FORCE" MENTIONS BY FILM

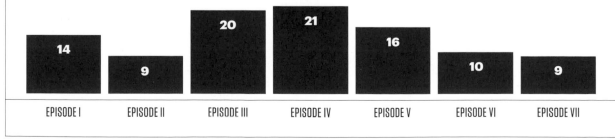

14	9	20	21	16	10	9
EPISODE I	EPISODE II	EPISODE III	EPISODE IV	EPISODE V	EPISODE VI	EPISODE VII

WITH THIS ONE

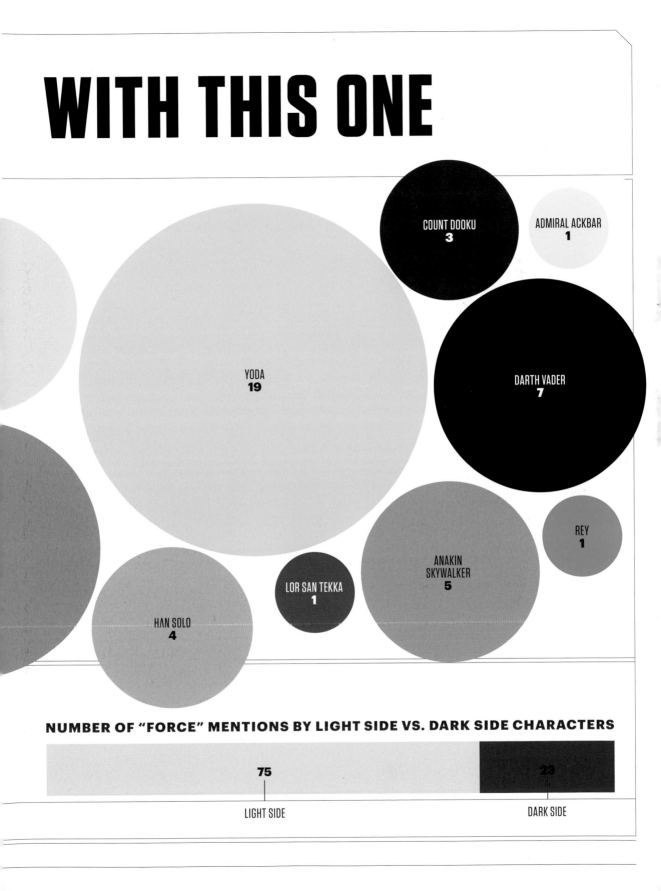

COUNT DOOKU
3

ADMIRAL ACKBAR
1

YODA
19

DARTH VADER
7

REY
1

ANAKIN
SKYWALKER
5

LOR SAN TEKKA
1

HAN SOLO
4

NUMBER OF "FORCE" MENTIONS BY LIGHT SIDE VS. DARK SIDE CHARACTERS

75

23

LIGHT SIDE

DARK SIDE

MORE POWER TO YOU

The Force gives those who can access it a variety of skills. Here's an analysis of who uses what skill.

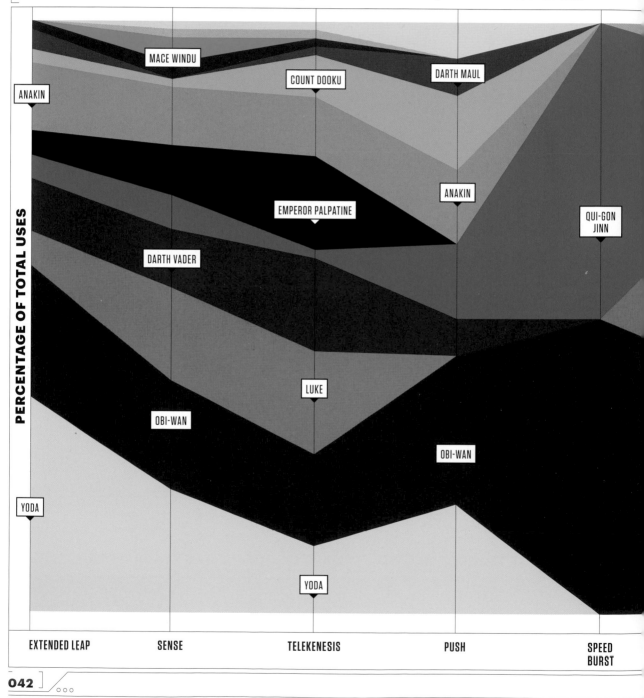

PERCENTAGE OF TOTAL USES

ANAKIN

MACE WINDU

COUNT DOOKU

DARTH MAUL

ANAKIN

EMPEROR PALPATINE

QUI-GON JINN

DARTH VADER

LUKE

OBI-WAN

OBI-WAN

YODA

YODA

EXTENDED LEAP · SENSE · TELEKENESIS · PUSH · SPEED BURST

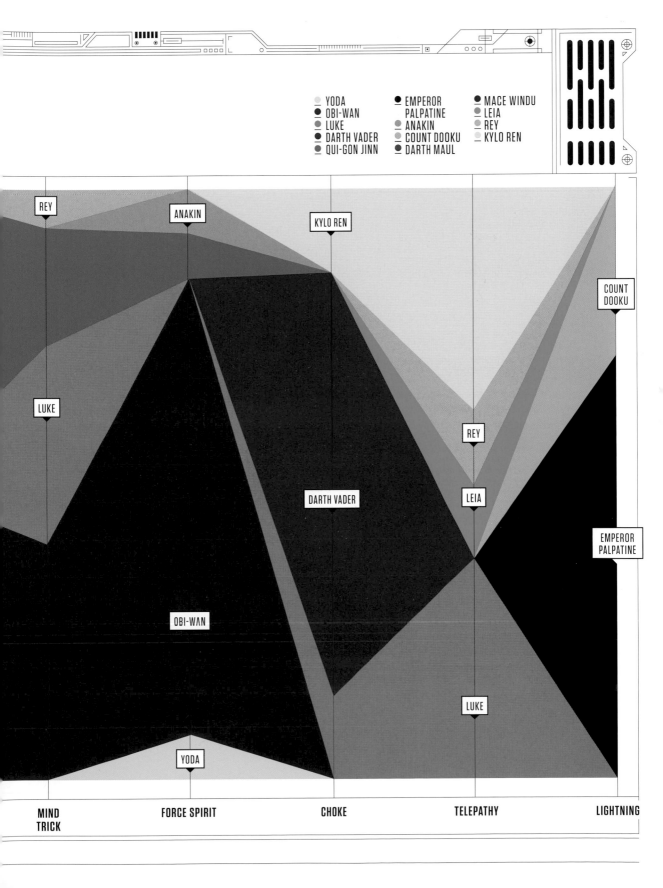

YODA
OBI-WAN
LUKE
DARTH VADER
QUI-GON JINN

EMPEROR
PALPATINE
ANAKIN
COUNT DOOKU
DARTH MAUL

MACE WINDU
LEIA
REY
KYLO REN

REY

ANAKIN

KYLO REN

COUNT
DOOKU

LUKE

REY

LEIA

DARTH VADER

EMPEROR
PALPATINE

OBI-WAN

LUKE

YODA

MIND
TRICK

FORCE SPIRIT

CHOKE

TELEPATHY

LIGHTNING

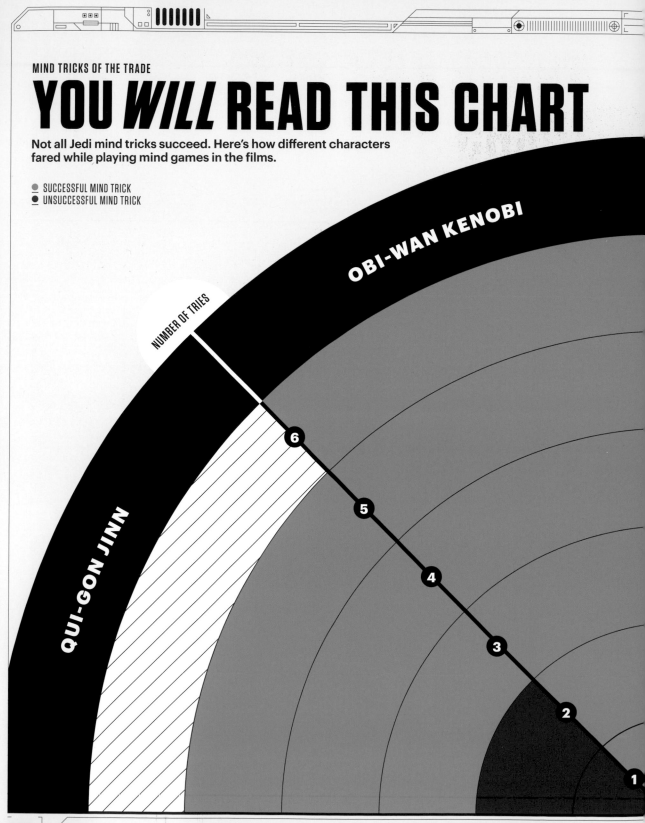

MIND TRICKS OF THE TRADE

YOU *WILL* READ THIS CHART

Not all Jedi mind tricks succeed. Here's how different characters fared while playing mind games in the films.

● SUCCESSFUL MIND TRICK
● UNSUCCESSFUL MIND TRICK

OBI-WAN KENOBI

NUMBER OF TRIES

QUI-GON JINN

6
5
4
3
2
1

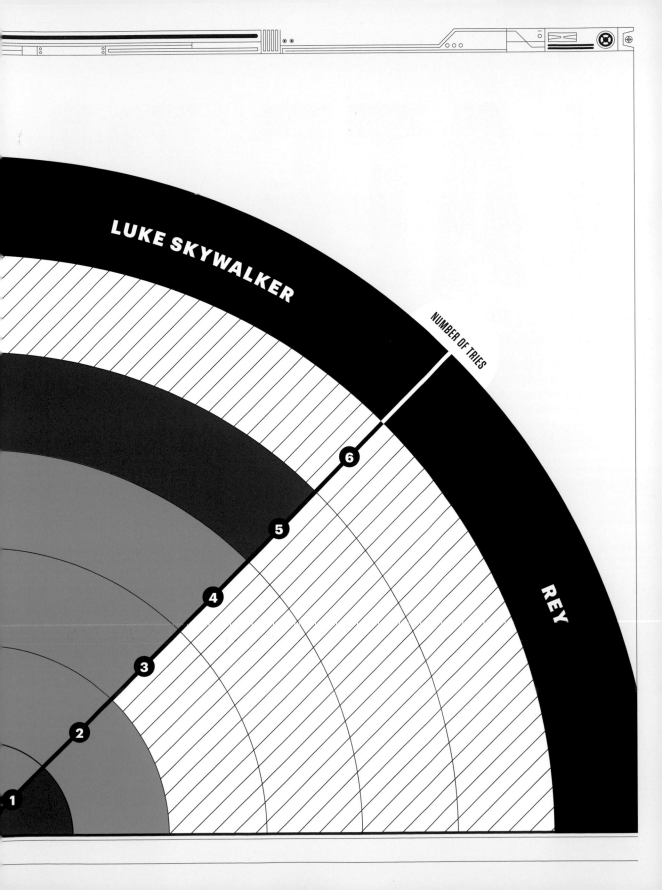

LUKE SKYWALKER

REY

NUMBER OF TRIES

1
2
3
4
5
6

LATE BL

Children are accepted as Jedi younglings between ages 3 and 6, but not some of your favorite characters. Here's the age they started their training.

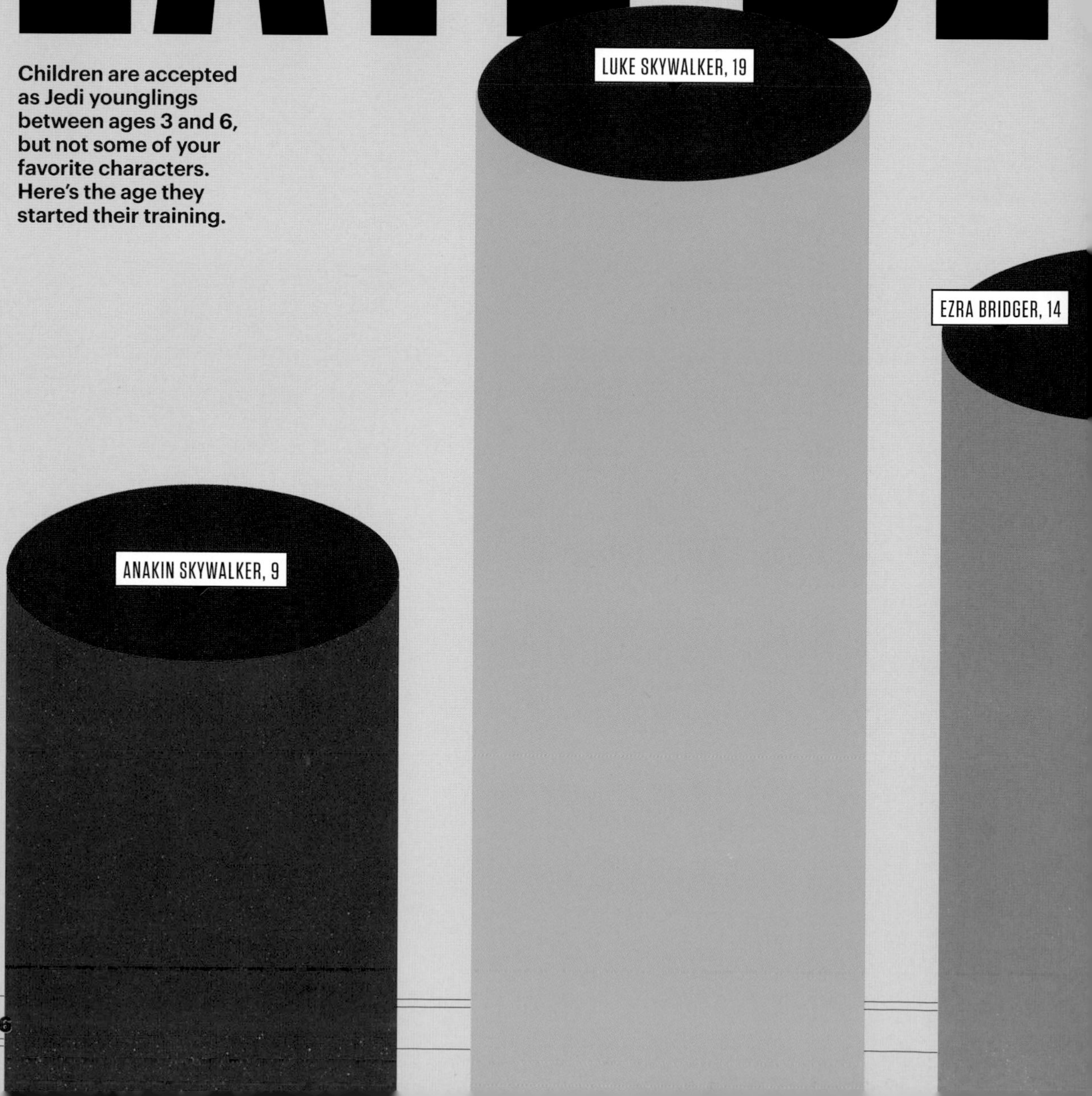

LUKE SKYWALKER, 19

EZRA BRIDGER, 14

ANAKIN SKYWALKER, 9

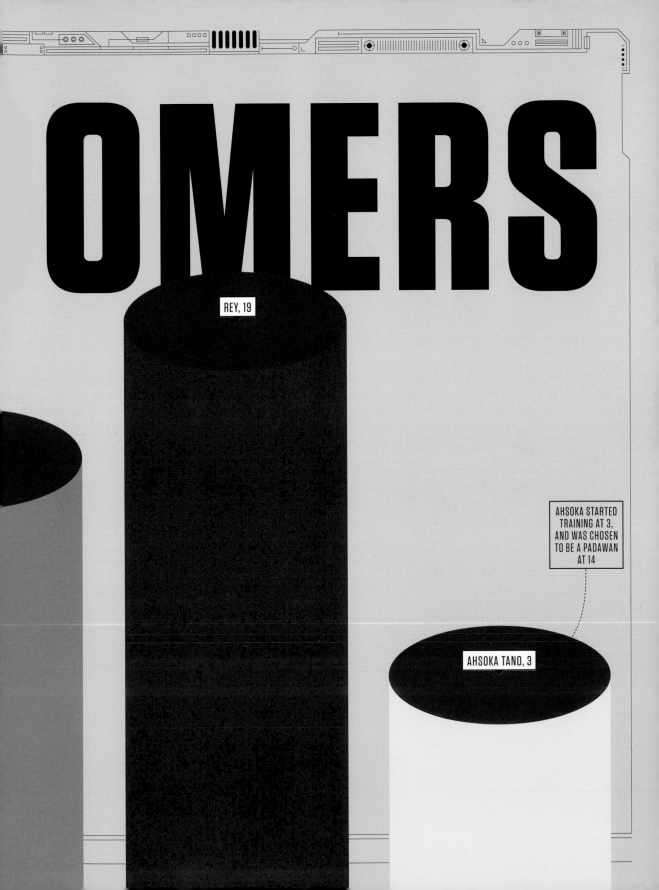

OMERS

REY, 19

AHSOKA STARTED
TRAINING AT 3,
AND WAS CHOSEN
TO BE A PADAWAN
AT 14

AHSOKA TANO, 3

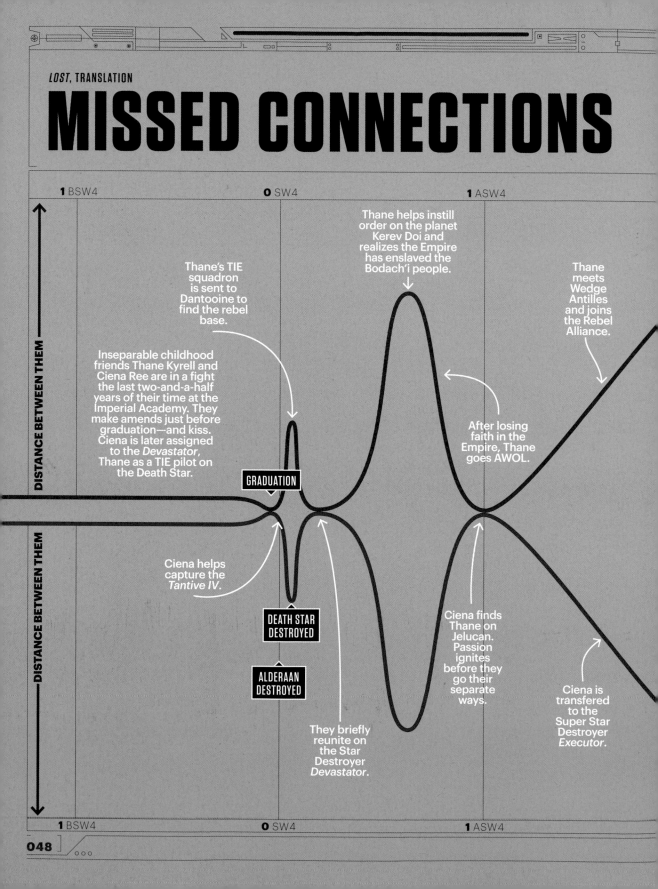

MISSED CONNECTIONS

DISTANCE BETWEEN THEM

DISTANCE BETWEEN THEM

1 BSW4

0 SW4

1 ASW4

Thane helps instill order on the planet Kerev Doi and realizes the Empire has enslaved the Bodach'i people.

Thane's TIE squadron is sent to Dantooine to find the rebel base.

Thane meets Wedge Antilles and joins the Rebel Alliance.

Inseparable childhood friends Thane Kyrell and Ciena Ree are in a fight the last two-and-a-half years of their time at the Imperial Academy. They make amends just before graduation—and kiss. Ciena is later assigned to the *Devastator*, Thane as a TIE pilot on the Death Star.

After losing faith in the Empire, Thane goes AWOL.

GRADUATION

Ciena helps capture the *Tantive IV*.

DEATH STAR DESTROYED

Ciena finds Thane on Jelucan. Passion ignites before they go their separate ways.

ALDERAAN DESTROYED

They briefly reunite on the Star Destroyer *Devastator*.

Ciena is transfered to the Super Star Destroyer *Executor*.

1 BSW4

0 SW4

1 ASW4

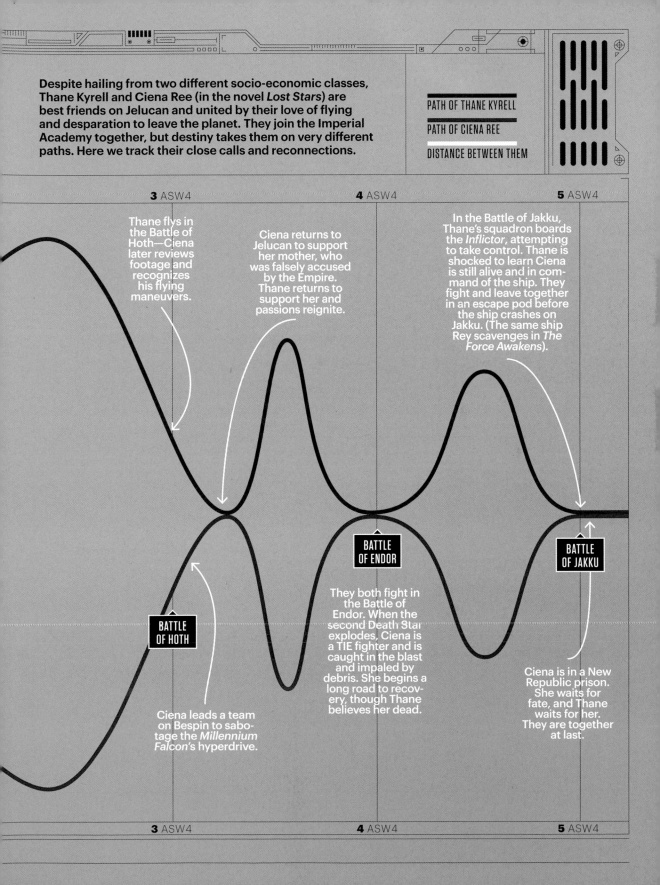

Despite hailing from two different socio-economic classes, Thane Kyrell and Ciena Ree (in the novel *Lost Stars*) are best friends on Jelucan and united by their love of flying and desparation to leave the planet. They join the Imperial Academy together, but destiny takes them on very different paths. Here we track their close calls and reconnections.

PATH OF THANE KYRELL

PATH OF CIENA REE

DISTANCE BETWEEN THEM

3 ASW4   **4** ASW4   **5** ASW4

Thane flys in the Battle of Hoth—Ciena later reviews footage and recognizes his flying maneuvers.

Ciena returns to Jelucan to support her mother, who was falsely accused by the Empire. Thane returns to support her and passions reignite.

In the Battle of Jakku, Thane's squadron boards the *Inflictor*, attempting to take control. Thane is shocked to learn Ciena is still alive and in command of the ship. They fight and leave together in an escape pod before the ship crashes on Jakku. (The same ship Rey scavenges in *The Force Awakens*).

BATTLE OF ENDOR

BATTLE OF HOTH

BATTLE OF JAKKU

They both fight in the Battle of Endor. When the second Death Star explodes, Ciena is a TIE fighter and is caught in the blast and impaled by debris. She begins a long road to recovery, though Thane believes her dead.

Ciena leads a team on Bespin to sabotage the *Millennium Falcon*'s hyperdrive.

Ciena is in a New Republic prison. She waits for fate, and Thane waits for her. They are together at last.

3 ASW4   **4** ASW4   **5** ASW4

JEDI HIGH COUNCIL SEATING CHART

The Jedi High Council consisted of twelve Jedi Masters who led the Jedi order and advised the Senate. Headquartered in Coruscant, the council convened in a circular chamber. The council consits of five permanent members, four long-term and three limited-term members.

ANAKIN SKYWALKER

COLEMAN KCAJ

SAESEE TIIN

OPPO RANCISIS

OPPO RANCISIS

SHAAK TI

SHAAK TI

SHAAK TI

KIT FISTO

SHAAK TI

KIT FISTO

KIT FISTO

KIT FISTO

ADI GALLIA

KIT FISTO

SHAAK TI

EETH KOTH

EETH KOTH

EETH KOTH

ADI GALLIA

OPPO RANCIS

EVEN

KIT FISTO

COLEMAN TREBOR

ADI GALLIA

OPPO RANCISIS

EV P

EETH KOTH

YARAEL POOF

ADI GALLIA

STASS ALLIE

COLEMAN KCAJ

COLEMAN KCAJ

DEPA BILLABA

EETH KOTH

DEPA BILLABA

| REVENGE OF THE SITH | THE CLONE WARS LEGACY | THE CLONE WARS SEASON 6 | THE CLONE WARS SEASON 5 | THE CLONE WARS SEASON 4 | ATTACK OF THE CLONES | THE PHANTOM MENACE |

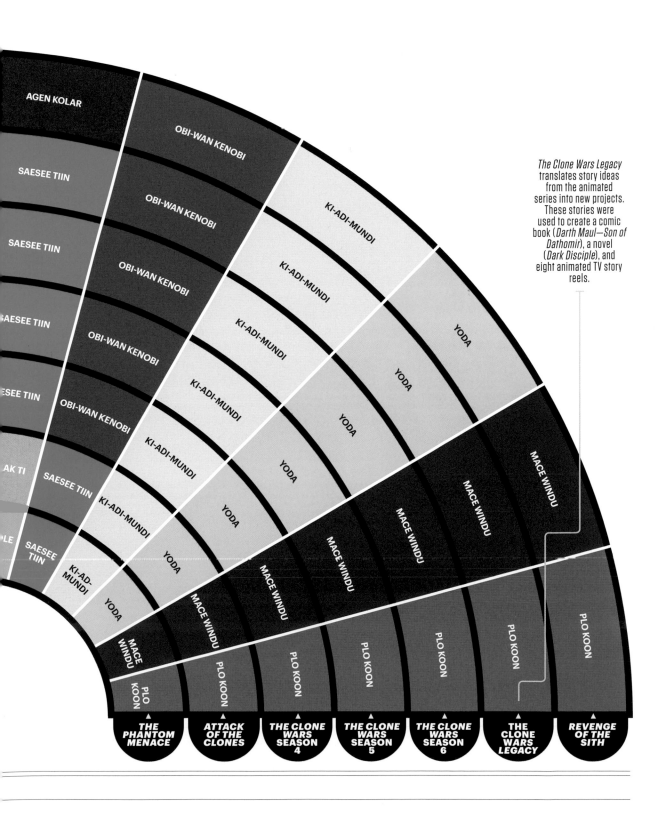

The Clone Wars Legacy translates story ideas from the animated series into new projects. These stories were used to create a comic book (*Darth Maul—Son of Dathomir*), a novel (*Dark Disciple*), and eight animated TV story reels.

AGEN KOLAR

SAESEE TIIN

SAESEE TIIN

SAESEE TIIN

SAESEE TIIN

SAESEE TIIN

AK TI

SAESEE TIIN

LE

SAESEE TIIN

OBI-WAN KENOBI

OBI-WAN KENOBI

OBI-WAN KENOBI

OBI-WAN KENOBI

OBI-WAN KENOBI

KI-ADI-MUNDI

KI-AD-MUNDI

KI-ADI-MUNDI

KI-ADI-MUNDI

KI-ADI-MUNDI

KI-ADI-MUNDI

KI-ADI-MUNDI

KI-ADI-MUNDI

YODA

YODA

YODA

YODA

YODA

YODA

YODA

YODA

MACE WINDU

MACE WINDU

MACE WINDU

MACE WINDU

MACE WINDU

MACE WINDU

MACE WINDU

MACE WINDU

PLO KOON

PLO KOON

PLO KOON

PLO KOON

PLO KOON

PLO KOON

PLO KOON

THE PHANTOM MENACE

ATTACK OF THE CLONES

THE CLONE WARS SEASON 4

THE CLONE WARS SEASON 5

THE CLONE WARS SEASON 6

THE CLONE WARS LEGACY

REVENGE OF THE SITH

THERE ARE OTHER JEDI

LED BY:
MASTER OF THE ORDER

THE JEDI HIGH COUNCIL

The Jedi High Council was composed of 12 members: five permanent, four long term, and three short term. This council functioned as the primary governing body of the Jedi.

THE COUNCIL OF REASSIGNMENT

Focusing on organization and personnel, this council oversaw the Jedi Service Corps. It also managed distribution and placement of Jedi Initiates who were not cut out to be Padawans. (Unknown number of members.)

COUNCILS?

LED BY:
CARETAKER OF FIRST KNOWLEDGE

THE COUNCIL OF FIRST KNOWLEDGE

This council's purview included the academy, its curriculum, as well as maintaining the Temple Archives.

THE COUNCIL OF RECONCILIATION

Focusing on diplomatic conflict resolution with the Galactic Senate and the Diplomatic Corps, the Council of Reconciliation, was made up of five members who specialized in negotiation and diplomacy.

THE ROAD TO *ROGUE*

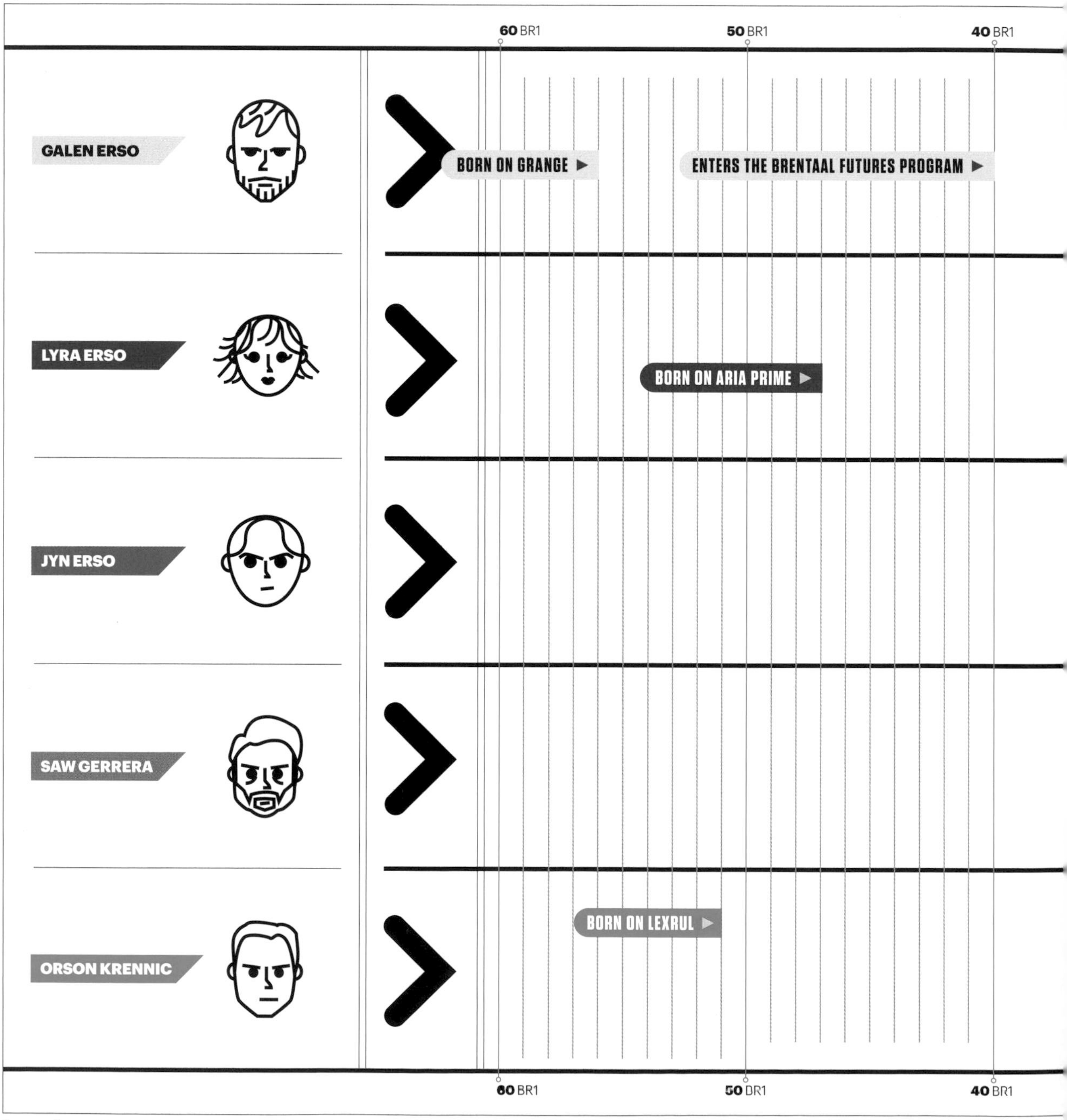

	60 BR1	**50** BR1	**40** BR1

GALEN ERSO

> BORN ON GRANGE ▶   ENTERS THE BRENTAAL FUTURES PROGRAM ▶

LYRA ERSO

> BORN ON ARIA PRIME ▶

JYN ERSO

>

SAW GERRERA

>

ORSON KRENNIC

> BORN ON LEXRUL ▶

	60 BR1	**50** DR1	**40** BR1

ONE

Catching up with key characters before *Rogue One*.

BR1 BEFORE *ROGUE ONE*

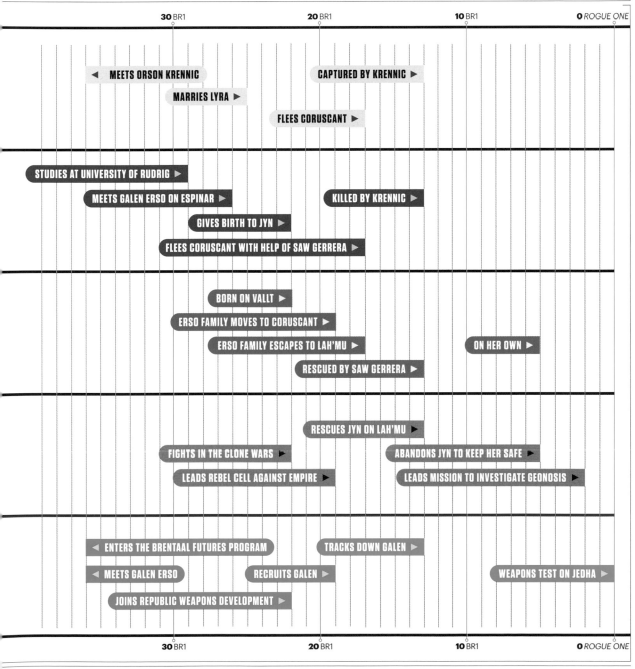

30 BR1   **20** BR1   **10** BR1   **0** *ROGUE ONE*

◄ MEETS ORSON KRENNIC   CAPTURED BY KRENNIC ►

MARRIES LYRA ►

FLEES CORUSCANT ►

STUDIES AT UNIVERSITY OF RUDRIG ►

MEETS GALEN ERSO ON ESPINAR ►   KILLED BY KRENNIC ►

GIVES BIRTH TO JYN ►

FLEES CORUSCANT WITH HELP OF SAW GERRERA ►

BORN ON VALLT ►

ERSO FAMILY MOVES TO CORUSCANT ►

ERSO FAMILY ESCAPES TO LAH'MU ►   ON HER OWN ►

RESCUED BY SAW GERRERA ►

RESCUES JYN ON LAH'MU ►

FIGHTS IN THE CLONE WARS ►   ABANDONS JYN TO KEEP HER SAFE ►

LEADS REBEL CELL AGAINST EMPIRE ►   LEADS MISSION TO INVESTIGATE GEONOSIS ►

◄ ENTERS THE BRENTAAL FUTURES PROGRAM   TRACKS DOWN GALEN ►

◄ MEETS GALEN ERSO   RECRUITS GALEN ►   WEAPONS TEST ON JEDHA ►

JOINS REPUBLIC WEAPONS DEVELOPMENT ►

30 BR1   **20** BR1   **10** BR1   **0** *ROGUE ONE*

ROLE REVERSAL

"The circle is now complete. When I left you, I was but the learner. Now I am the master."
—DARTH VADER TO OBI-WAN

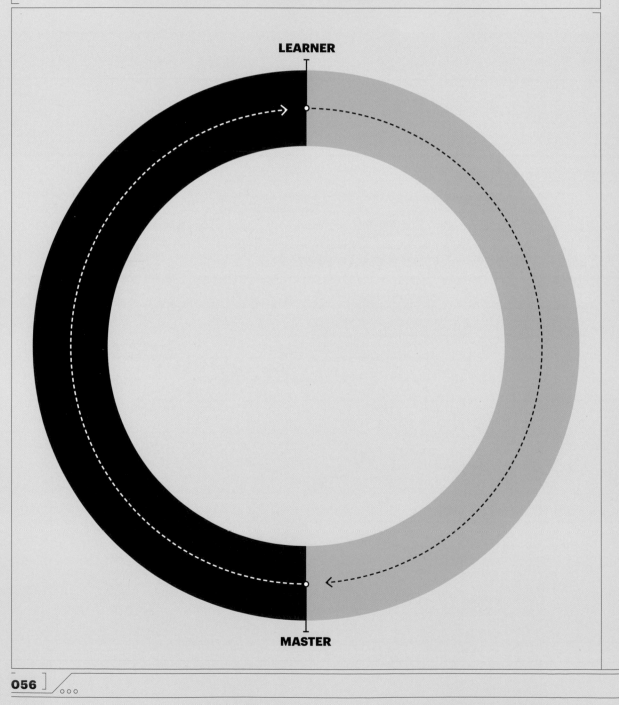

LEARNER

MASTER

DOUBLE FEATURES

Characters with extra organs.

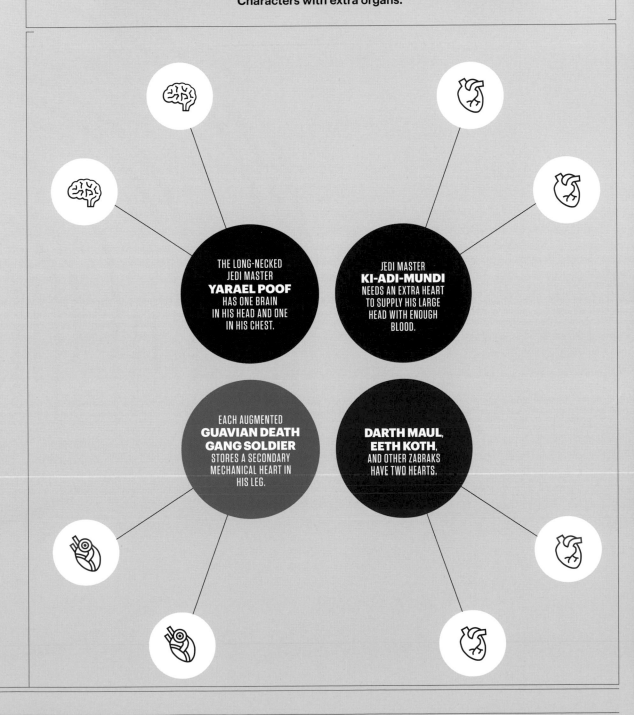

THE LONG-NECKED JEDI MASTER **YARAEL POOF** HAS ONE BRAIN IN HIS HEAD AND ONE IN HIS CHEST.

JEDI MASTER **KI-ADI-MUNDI** NEEDS AN EXTRA HEART TO SUPPLY HIS LARGE HEAD WITH ENOUGH BLOOD.

EACH AUGMENTED **GUAVIAN DEATH GANG SOLDIER** STORES A SECONDARY MECHANICAL HEART IN HIS LEG.

DARTH MAUL, EETH KOTH, AND OTHER ZABRAKS HAVE TWO HEARTS.

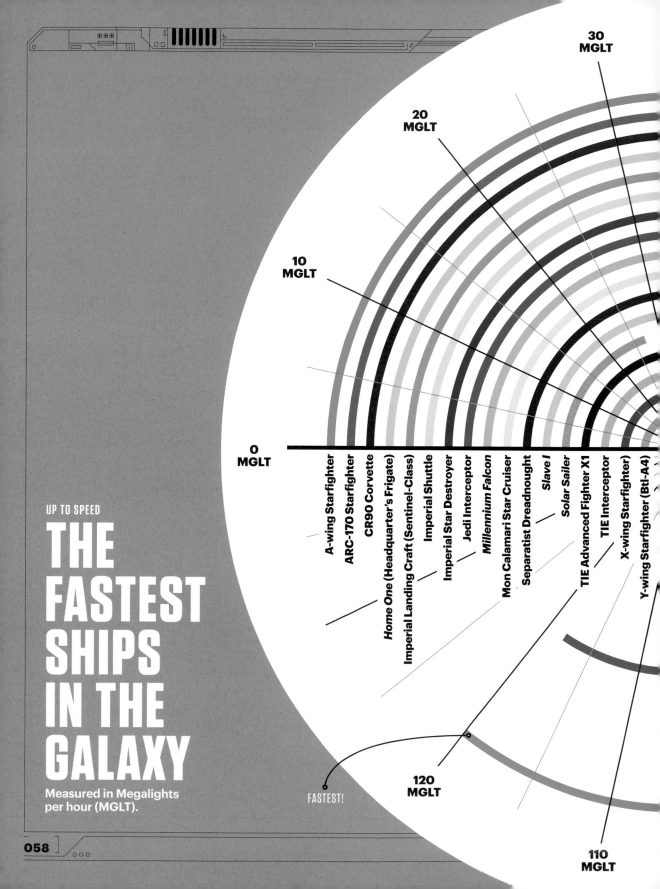

THE FASTEST SHIPS IN THE GALAXY

Measured in Megalights per hour (MGLT).

0 MGLT

10 MGLT

20 MGLT

30 MGLT

120 MGLT

110 MGLT

FASTEST!

A-wing Starfighter

ARC-170 Starfighter

CR90 Corvette

Home One (Headquarter's Frigate)

Imperial Landing Craft (Sentinel-Class)

Imperial Shuttle

Imperial Star Destroyer

Jedi Interceptor

Millennium Falcon

Mon Calamari Star Cruiser

Separatist Dreadnought

Slave I

Solar Sailer

TIE Advanced Fighter X1

TIE Interceptor

X-wing Starfighter

Y-wing Starfighter (Btl-A4)

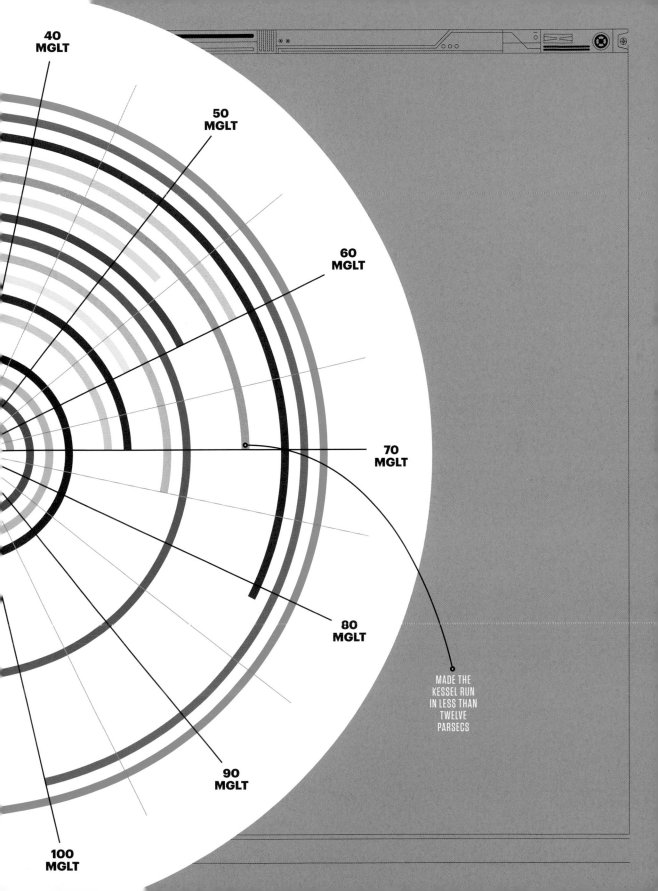

40
MGLT

50
MGLT

60
MGLT

70
MGLT

80
MGLT

90
MGLT

100
MGLT

MADE THE
KESSEL RUN
IN LESS THAN
TWELVE
PARSECS

WHO HAS THE *MILLENNIUM FALCON*?

HAN WINS THE *FALCON* IN A GAME OF SABACC AGAINST LANDO

HAN LETS LANDO BORROW THE *FALCON* DURING THE BATTLE OF ENDOR

HAN GETS THE *FALCON* BACK FROM LANDO AFTER THE BATTLE OF ENDOR

HAN SOMEHOW LOSES THE *FALCON*

THE IRVING BOYS STEAL THE *FALCON* FROM DUCAIN

LANDO CALRISSIAN

HAN SOLO

LANDO CALRISSIAN

HAN SOLO

GANNIS DUCAIN

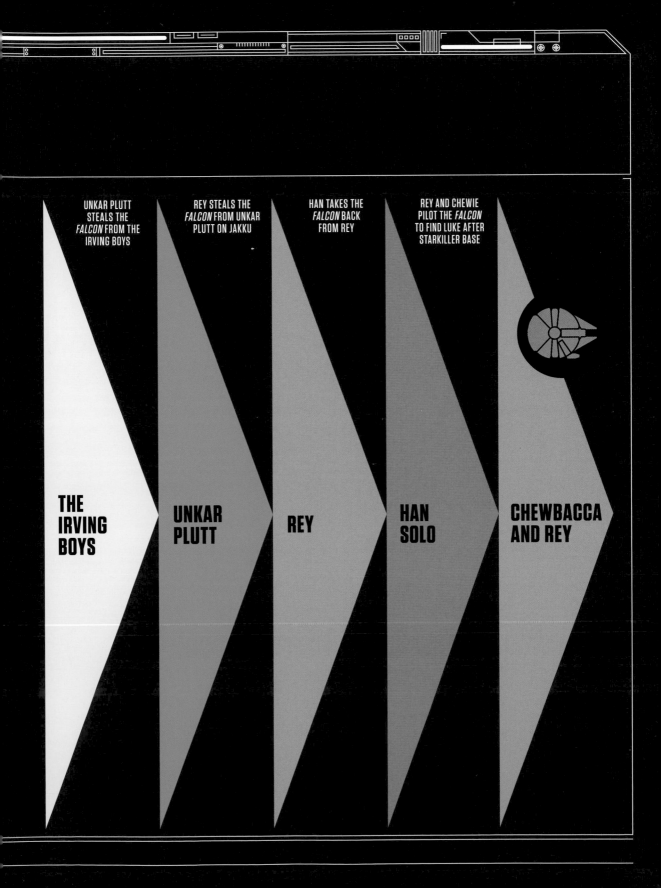

UNKAR PLUTT
STEALS THE
FALCON FROM THE
IRVING BOYS

REY STEALS THE
FALCON FROM UNKAR
PLUTT ON JAKKU

HAN TAKES THE
FALCON BACK
FROM REY

REY AND CHEWIE
PILOT THE *FALCON*
TO FIND LUKE AFTER
STARKILLER BASE

THE
IRVING
BOYS

UNKAR
PLUTT

REY

HAN
SOLO

CHEWBACCA
AND REY

TIE GAME

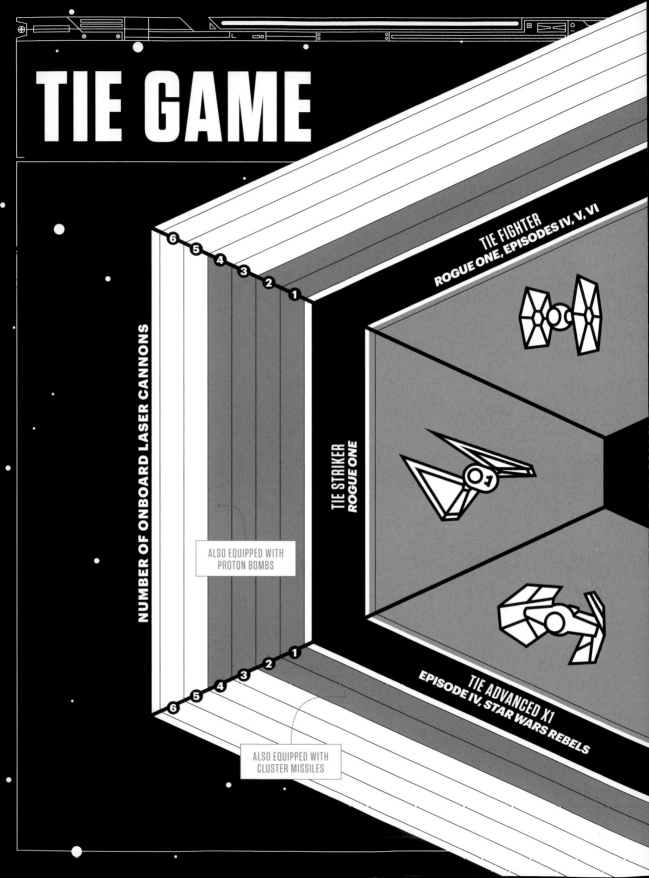

NUMBER OF ONBOARD LASER CANNONS

6 5 4 3 2 1

TIE FIGHTER
ROGUE ONE, EPISODES IV, V, VI

TIE STRIKER
ROGUE ONE

ALSO EQUIPPED WITH
PROTON BOMBS

1 2 3 4 5 6

TIE ADVANCED X1
EPISODE IV, STAR WARS REBELS

ALSO EQUIPPED WITH
CLUSTER MISSILES

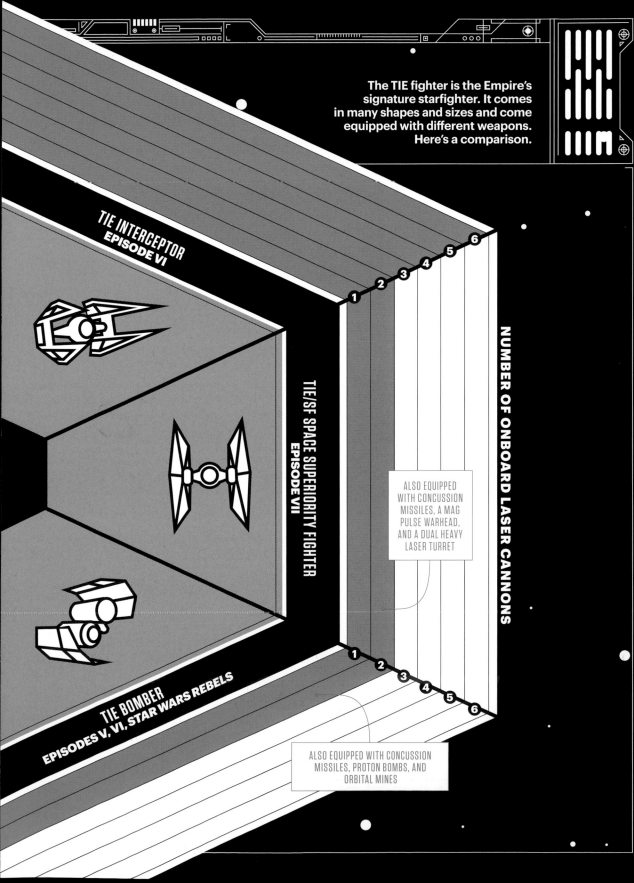

The TIE fighter is the Empire's signature starfighter. It comes in many shapes and sizes and come equipped with different weapons. Here's a comparison.

TIE INTERCEPTOR
EPISODE VI

TIE/SF SPACE SUPERIORITY FIGHTER
EPISODE VII

TIE BOMBER
EPISODES V, VI, STAR WARS REBELS

NUMBER OF ONBOARD LASER CANNONS

1 2 3 4 5 6

ALSO EQUIPPED WITH CONCUSSION MISSILES, A MAG PULSE WARHEAD, AND A DUAL HEAVY LASER TURRET

1 2 3 4 5 6

ALSO EQUIPPED WITH CONCUSSION MISSILES, PROTON BOMBS, AND ORBITAL MINES

CONSTRUCTING THE DEATH STAR

BSW4 BEFORE *STAR WARS*: EPISODE IV *A NEW HOPE*
ASW4 AFTER *STAR WARS*: EPISODE IV *A NEW HOPE*

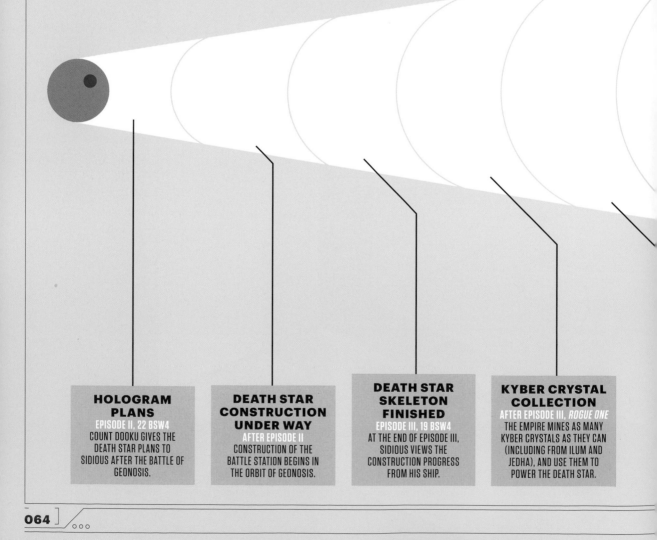

HOLOGRAM PLANS
EPISODE II, 22 BSW4
COUNT DOOKU GIVES THE DEATH STAR PLANS TO SIDIOUS AFTER THE BATTLE OF GEONOSIS.

DEATH STAR CONSTRUCTION UNDER WAY
AFTER EPISODE II
CONSTRUCTION OF THE BATTLE STATION BEGINS IN THE ORBIT OF GEONOSIS.

DEATH STAR SKELETON FINISHED
EPISODE III, 19 BSW4
AT THE END OF EPISODE III, SIDIOUS VIEWS THE CONSTRUCTION PROGRESS FROM HIS SHIP.

KYBER CRYSTAL COLLECTION
AFTER EPISODE III, *ROGUE ONE*
THE EMPIRE MINES AS MANY KYBER CRYSTALS AS THEY CAN (INCLUDING FROM ILUM AND JEDHA), AND USE THEM TO POWER THE DEATH STAR.

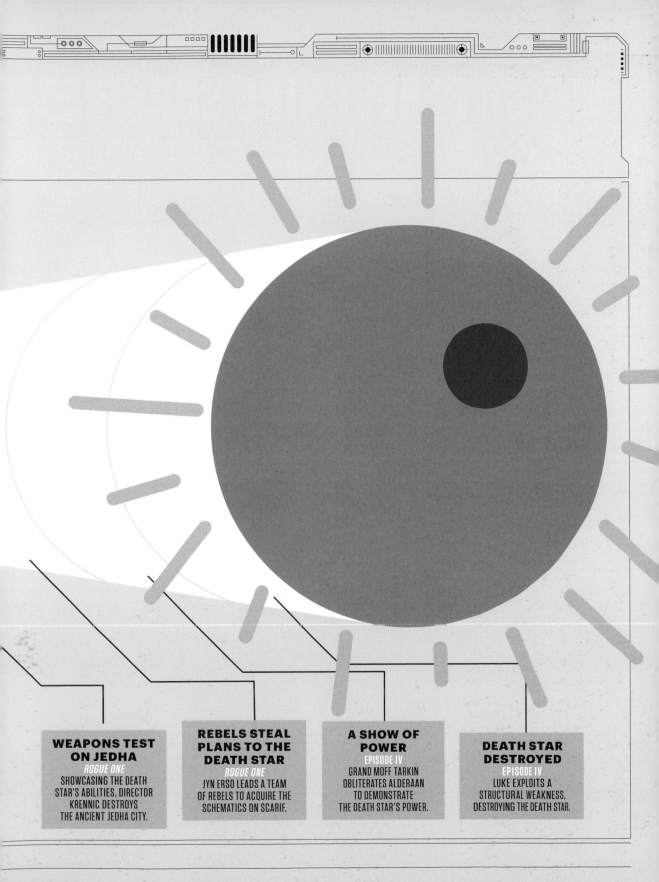

WEAPONS TEST ON JEDHA
ROGUE ONE
SHOWCASING THE DEATH STAR'S ABILITIES, DIRECTOR KRENNIC DESTROYS THE ANCIENT JEDHA CITY.

REBELS STEAL PLANS TO THE DEATH STAR
ROGUE ONE
JYN ERSO LEADS A TEAM OF REBELS TO ACQUIRE THE SCHEMATICS ON SCARIF.

A SHOW OF POWER
EPISODE IV
GRAND MOFF TARKIN OBLITERATES ALDERAAN TO DEMONSTRATE THE DEATH STAR'S POWER.

DEATH STAR DESTROYED
EPISODE IV
LUKE EXPLOITS A STRUCTURAL WEAKNESS, DESTROYING THE DEATH STAR.

WHICH REBEL SHIPS SURVIVED

RESULT	△ KILLED IN ACTION	▲ SURVIVED

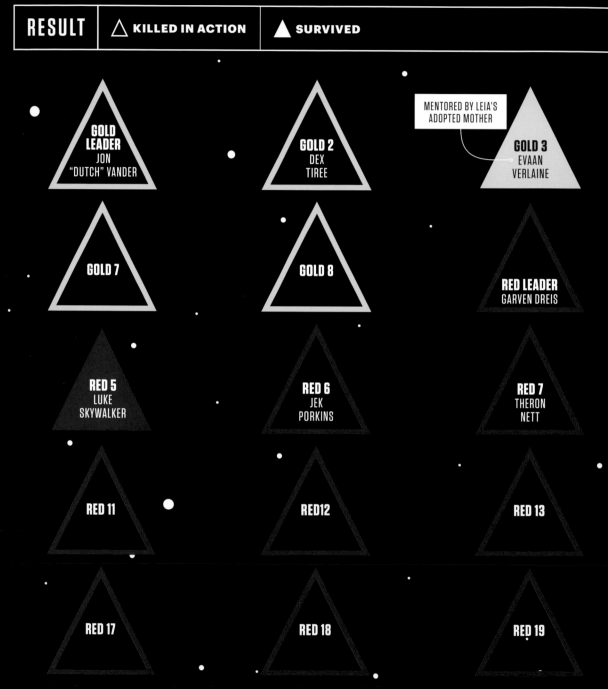

△ **GOLD LEADER**
JON "DUTCH" VANDER

△ **GOLD 2**
DEX TIREE

MENTORED BY LEIA'S ADOPTED MOTHER

▲ **GOLD 3**
EVAAN VERLAINE

△ **GOLD 7**

△ **GOLD 8**

△ **RED LEADER**
GARVEN DREIS

▲ **RED 5**
LUKE SKYWALKER

△ **RED 6**
JEK PORKINS

△ **RED 7**
THERON NETT

△ **RED 11**

△ **RED12**

△ **RED 13**

△ **RED 17**

△ **RED 18**

△ **RED 19**

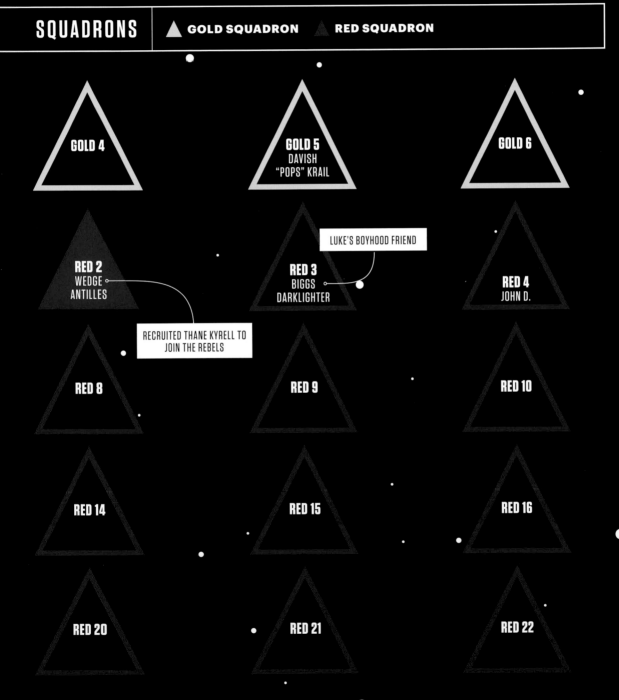

THE BATTLE OF YAVIN

How the outmatched rebel fleet fared in the battle against the first Death Star.

SQUADRONS   ▲ GOLD SQUADRON   ▲ RED SQUADRON

GOLD 4

GOLD 5
DAVISH
"POPS" KRAIL

GOLD 6

LUKE'S BOYHOOD FRIEND

RED 2
WEDGE
ANTILLES

RED 3
BIGGS
DARKLIGHTER

RED 4
JOHN D.

RECRUITED THANE KYRELL TO
JOIN THE REBELS

RED 8

RED 9

RED 10

RED 14

RED 15

RED 16

RED 20

RED 21

RED 22

DISMEMBERS ONLY

STAR WARS:
EPISODE I
*THE PHANTOM
MENACE*
IS THE ONLY
FILM WHERE NO
ONE LOSES AN
ARM. LEGS ARE
ANOTHER STORY.
SORRY,
DARTH MAUL.

ZAM WESELL

WHEN
Episode II
HOW
Obi-Wan strikes
down the
shapeshifting
assassin as
she sneaks up
behind him
in a bar.

THE ACKLAY

WHEN
Episode II
HOW
In the arena bat-
tle at Geonosis,
Obi-Wan cuts
off two of the
acklay's giant
arms before
delivering a
killstroke.

ANAKIN SKYWALKER

WHEN
Episode II
HOW
After the battle
of Geonosis,
Anakin and
Obi-Wan follow
Count Dooku.
Obi-Wan is
knocked out and
Anakin loses an
arm to Dooku.

COUNT DOOKU

WHEN
Episode III
HOW
Anakin and
Obi-Wan again
hunt down
Dooku. Obi-Wan
is knocked
out again, but
Anakin cuts off
both of Dooku's
hands, before
also removing
his head.

GENERAL GRIEVOUS

WHEN
Episode III
HOW
Obi-Wan cuts
off two of the
lightsaber-
wielding
cyborg's four
hands.

MACE WINDU

WHEN
Episode III
HOW
Anakin cuts
off Windu's
hand to protect
Darth Sidious.
Sidious, in turn,
launches Windu
out the window.

ANAKIN SKYWALKER

WHEN
Episode III
HOW
In the battle
on Mustafar,
Obi-Wan cuts
off Anakin's arm
and both legs.

Raise your hand if you remember Luke Skywalker losing an appendage in *The Empire Strikes Back*. But do you remember all the other times someone has lost an arm or hand in the films? Here's everyone who contributed to the arms race.

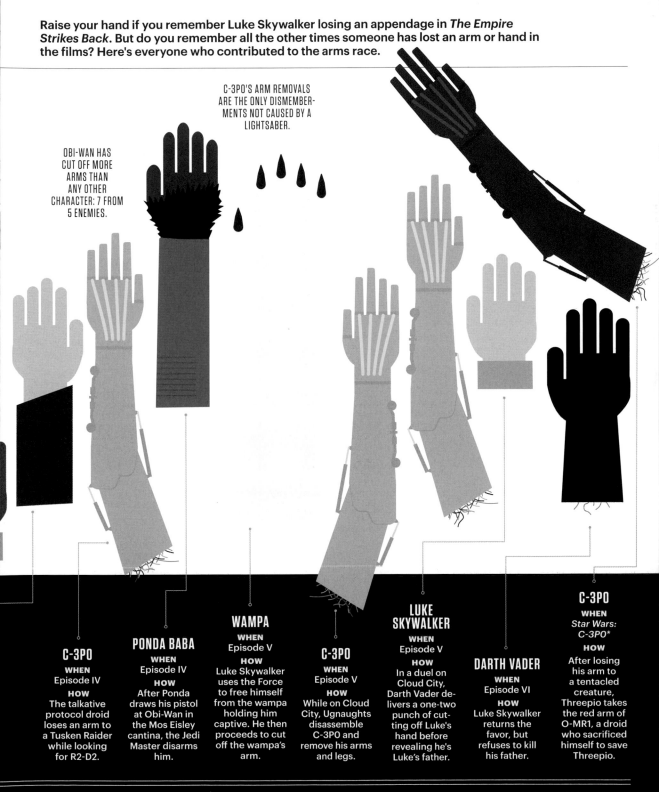

C-3PO'S ARM REMOVALS ARE THE ONLY DISMEMBER-MENTS NOT CAUSED BY A LIGHTSABER.

OBI-WAN HAS CUT OFF MORE ARMS THAN ANY OTHER CHARACTER: 7 FROM 5 ENEMIES.

C-3PO
WHEN
Episode IV
HOW
The talkative protocol droid loses an arm to a Tusken Raider while looking for R2-D2.

PONDA BABA
WHEN
Episode IV
HOW
After Ponda draws his pistol at Obi-Wan in the Mos Eisley cantina, the Jedi Master disarms him.

WAMPA
WHEN
Episode V
HOW
Luke Skywalker uses the Force to free himself from the wampa holding him captive. He then proceeds to cut off the wampa's arm.

C-3PO
WHEN
Episode V
HOW
While on Cloud City, Ugnaughts disassemble C-3PO and remove his arms and legs.

LUKE SKYWALKER
WHEN
Episode V
HOW
In a duel on Cloud City, Darth Vader de-livers a one-two punch of cut-ting off Luke's hand before revealing he's Luke's father.

DARTH VADER
WHEN
Episode VI
HOW
Luke Skywalker returns the favor, but refuses to kill his father.

C-3PO
WHEN
Star Wars: C-3PO*
HOW
After losing his arm to a tentacled creature, Threepio takes the red arm of O-MR1, a droid who sacrificed himself to save Threepio.

* *COMIC BOOK, NOT A FILM*

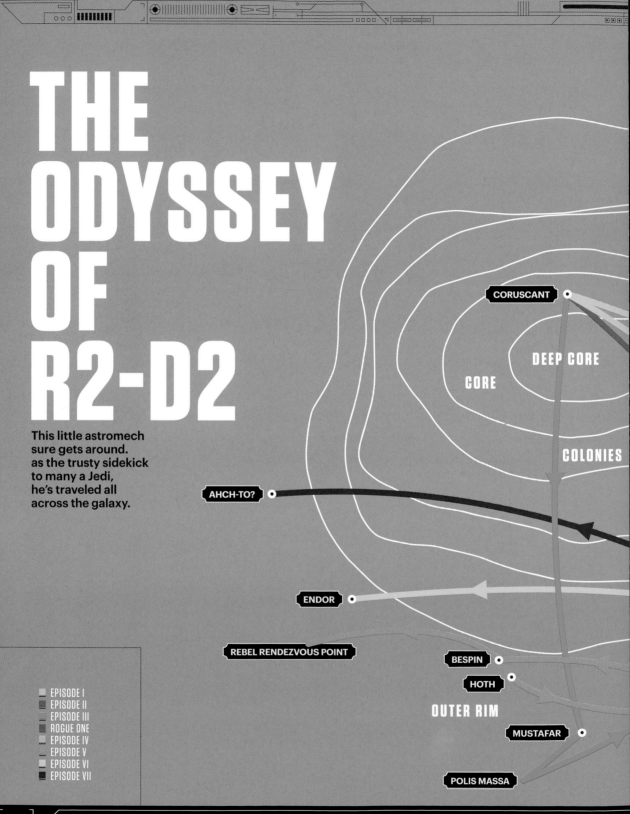

THE ODYSSEY OF R2-D2

This little astromech sure gets around. as the trusty sidekick to many a Jedi, he's traveled all across the galaxy.

CORUSCANT

DEEP CORE

CORE

COLONIES

AHCH-TO?

ENDOR

REBEL RENDEZVOUS POINT

BESPIN

HOTH

OUTER RIM

MUSTAFAR

POLIS MASSA

EPISODE I
EPISODE II
EPISODE III
ROGUE ONE
EPISODE IV
EPISODE V
EPISODE VI
EPISODE VII

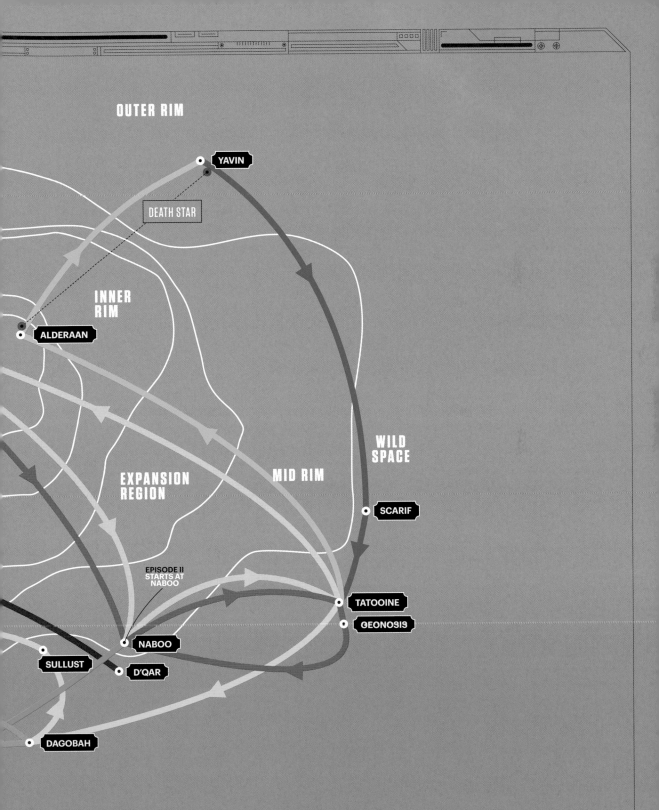

OUTER RIM

YAVIN

DEATH STAR

INNER
RIM

ALDERAAN

WILD
SPACE

EXPANSION
REGION

MID RIM

SCARIF

EPISODE II
STARTS AT
NABOO

TATOOINE

GEONOSIS

NABOO

SULLUST

D'QAR

DAGOBAH

THE FIVE DROID CLASSIFICATIONS

Every type of droid fits into one of five distinct categories. (Yes, even R2-D2).

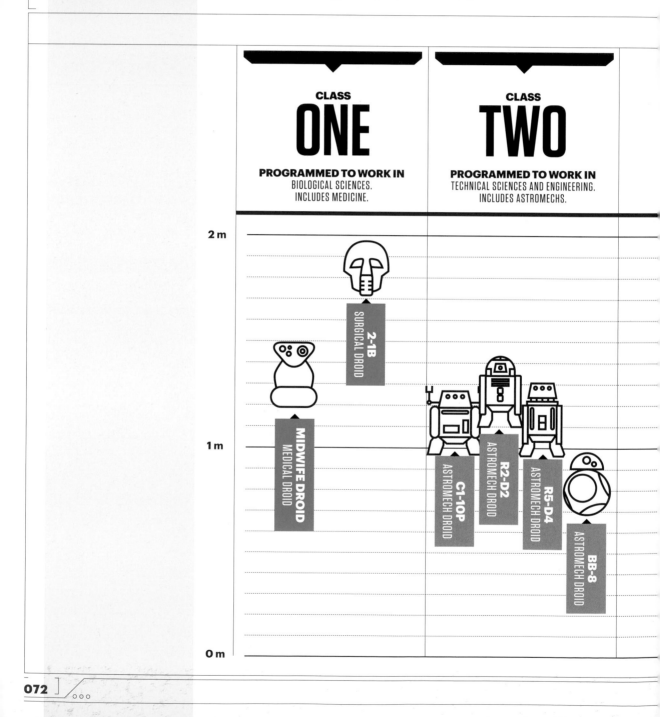

CLASS

ONE

PROGRAMMED TO WORK IN
BIOLOGICAL SCIENCES.
INCLUDES MEDICINE.

CLASS

TWO

PROGRAMMED TO WORK IN
TECHNICAL SCIENCES AND ENGINEERING.
INCLUDES ASTROMECHS.

2 m

1 m

0 m

2-1B
SURGICAL DROID

MIDWIFE DROID
MEDICAL DROID

C1-10P
ASTROMECH DROID

R2-D2
ASTROMECH DROID

R5-D4
ASTROMECH DROID

BB-8
ASTROMECH DROID

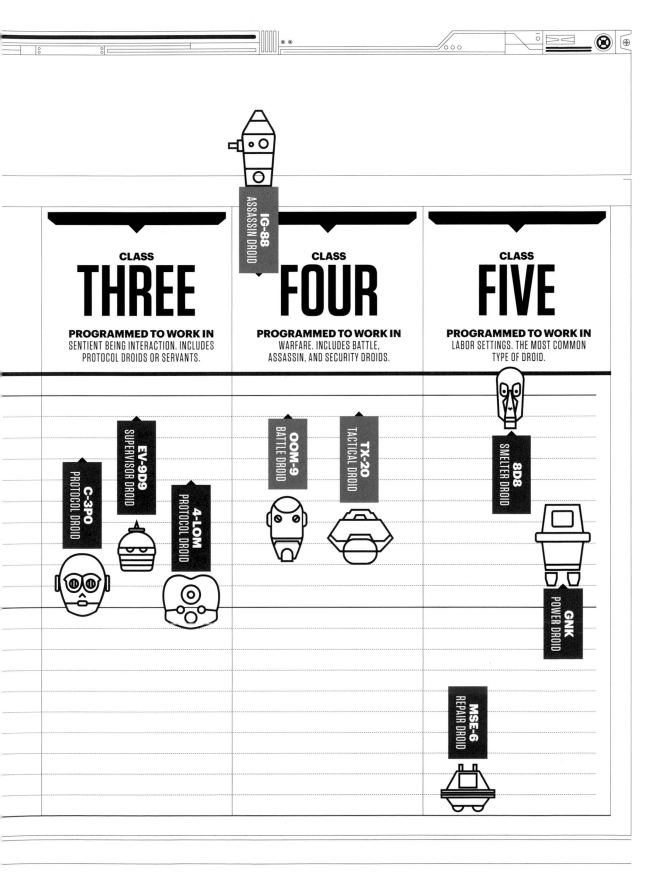

IG-88
ASSASSIN DROID

CLASS
THREE
PROGRAMMED TO WORK IN
SENTIENT BEING INTERACTION. INCLUDES
PROTOCOL DROIDS OR SERVANTS.

CLASS
FOUR
PROGRAMMED TO WORK IN
WARFARE. INCLUDES BATTLE,
ASSASSIN, AND SECURITY DROIDS.

CLASS
FIVE
PROGRAMMED TO WORK IN
LABOR SETTINGS. THE MOST COMMON
TYPE OF DROID.

EV-9D9
SUPERVISOR DROID

C-3PO
PROTOCOL DROID

4-LOM
PROTOCOL DROID

OOM-9
BATTLE DROID

TX-20
TACTICAL DROID

8D8
SMELTER DROID

GNK
POWER DROID

MSE-6
REPAIR DROID

WHAT R2-D2 IS THINKING

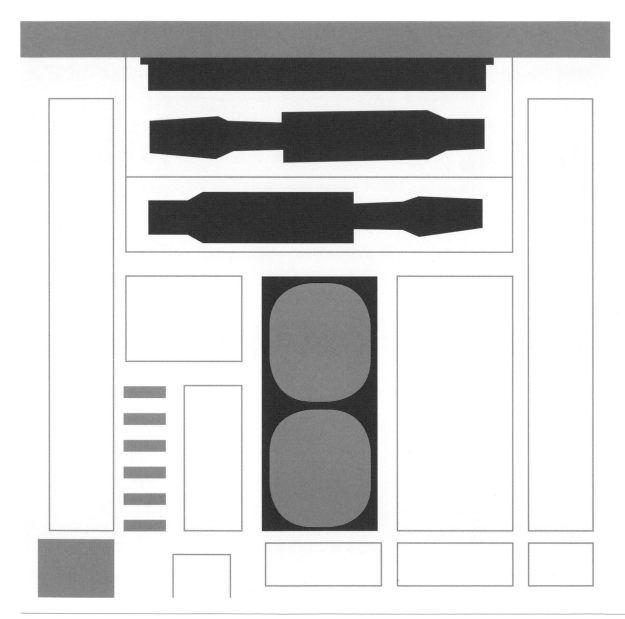

○ BEEP
● BOOP
● BLEEP

WHAT C-3PO IS THINKING

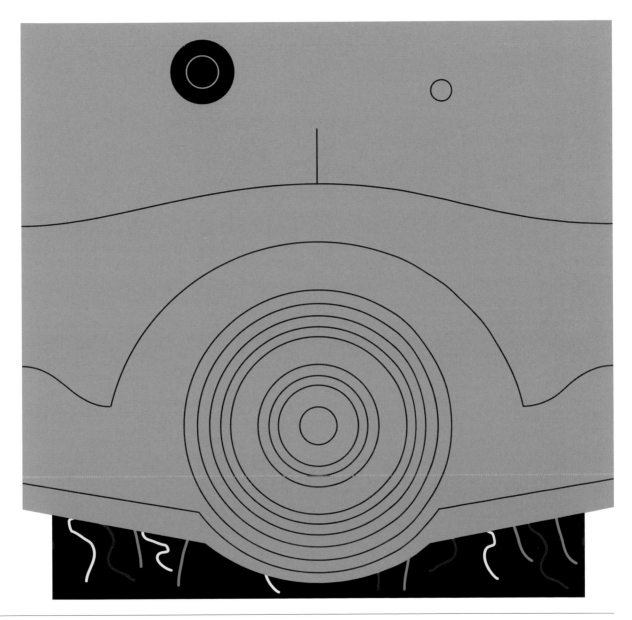

- WE'RE DOOMED!
- GOODNESS GRACIOUS ME
- OH, MY

3,720 to 1

DROID PERSONALITY

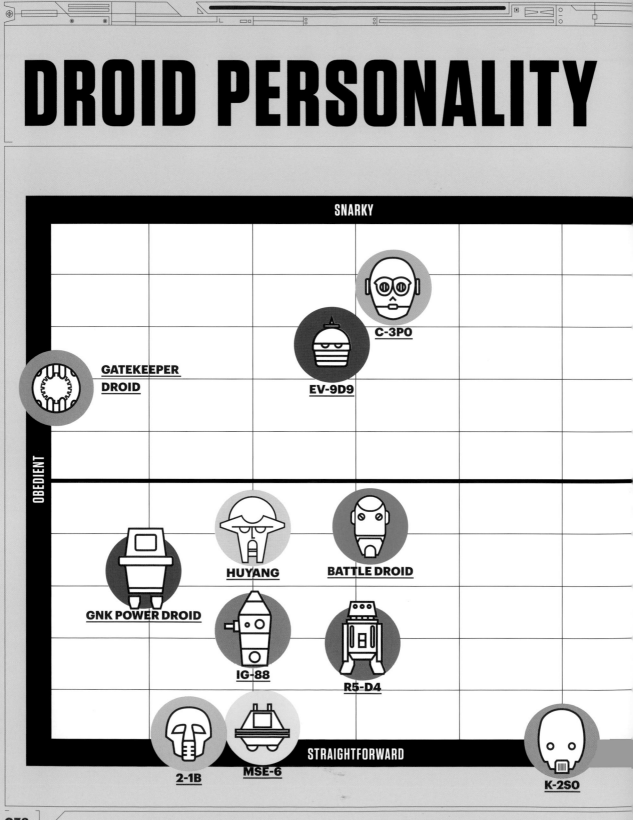

SNARKY

C-3PO

EV-9D9

GATEKEEPER DROID

OBEDIENT

HUYANG

BATTLE DROID

GNK POWER DROID

IG-88

R5-D4

2-1B

MSE-6

STRAIGHTFORWARD

K-2SO

MATRIX

Not all droids are programmed equally. Some are, ahem, rebels (Chopper!), while some are more obedient.

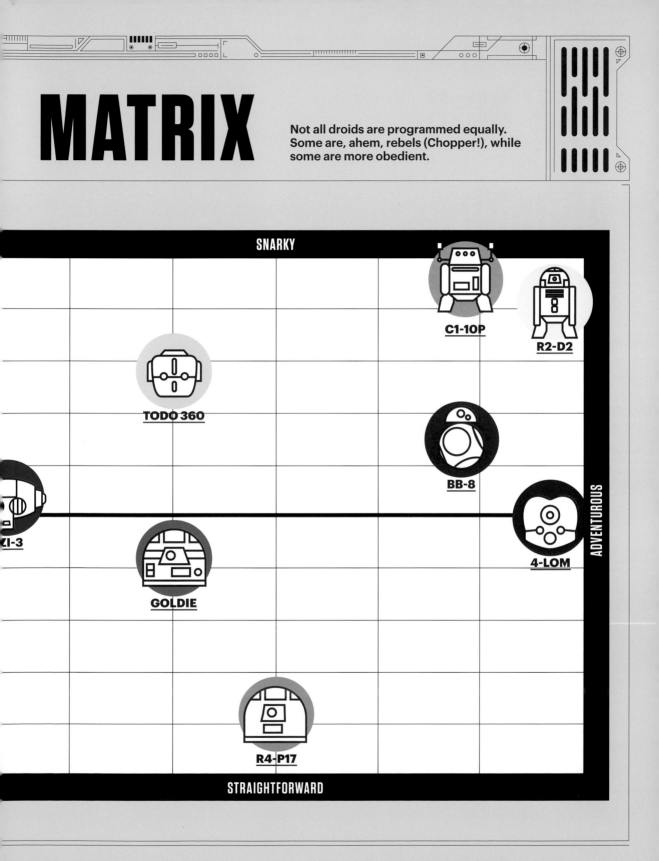

SNARKY

C1-10P

R2-D2

TODO 360

BB-8

XI-3

GOLDIE

4-LOM

ADVENTUROUS

R4-P17

STRAIGHTFORWARD

HOW BB-8 GETS AROUND

◻ ROLLS
▨ STABILIZING HOOKS

BATTLE DROID RESPONSES

■ ROGER
■ ROGER, ROGER

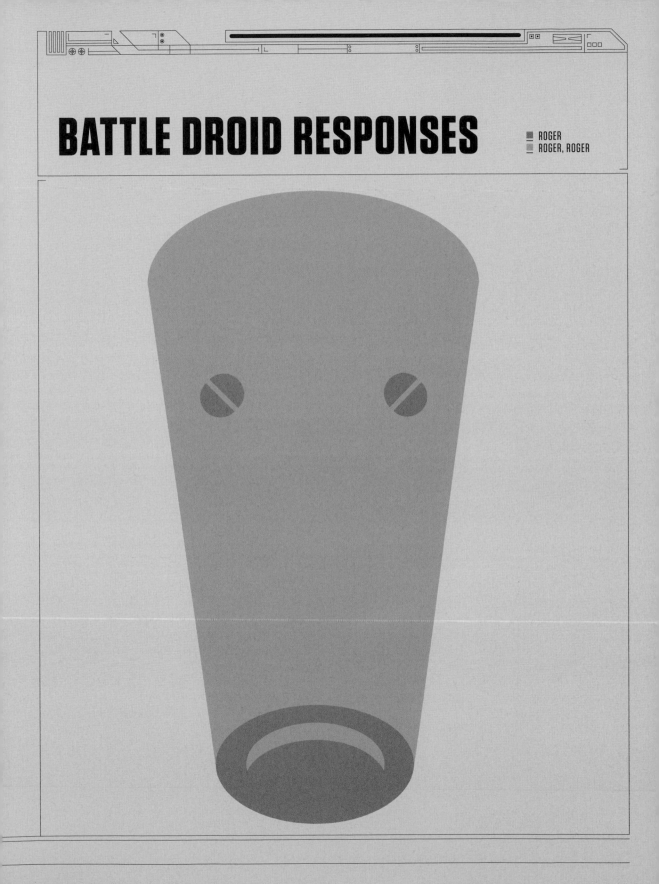

DROID RAGE

The Jedi warriors that killed the most droids in the second battle of Geonosis (*The Clone Wars*).

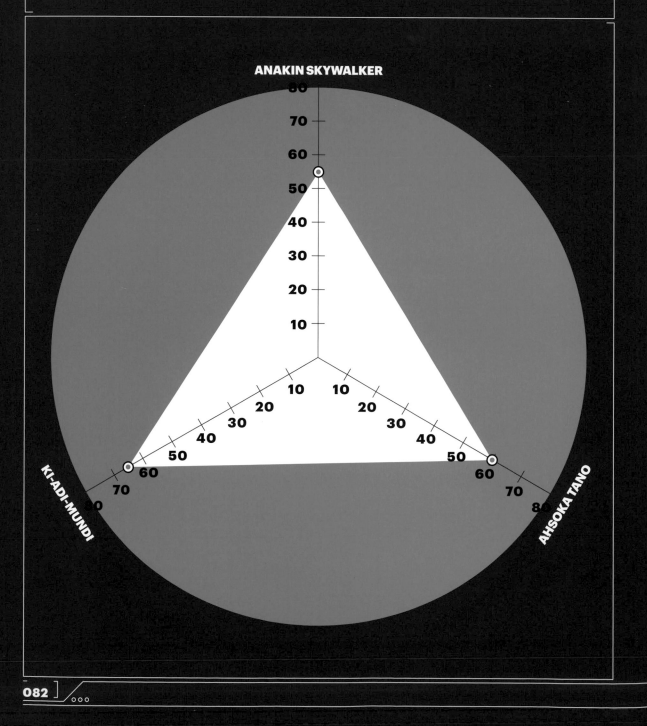

ANAKIN SKYWALKER

KI-ADI-MUNDI

AHSOKA TANO

DARTH VADER

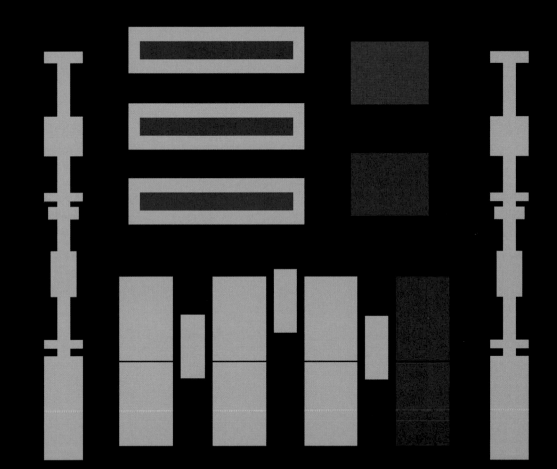

MEET THE *REBELS*

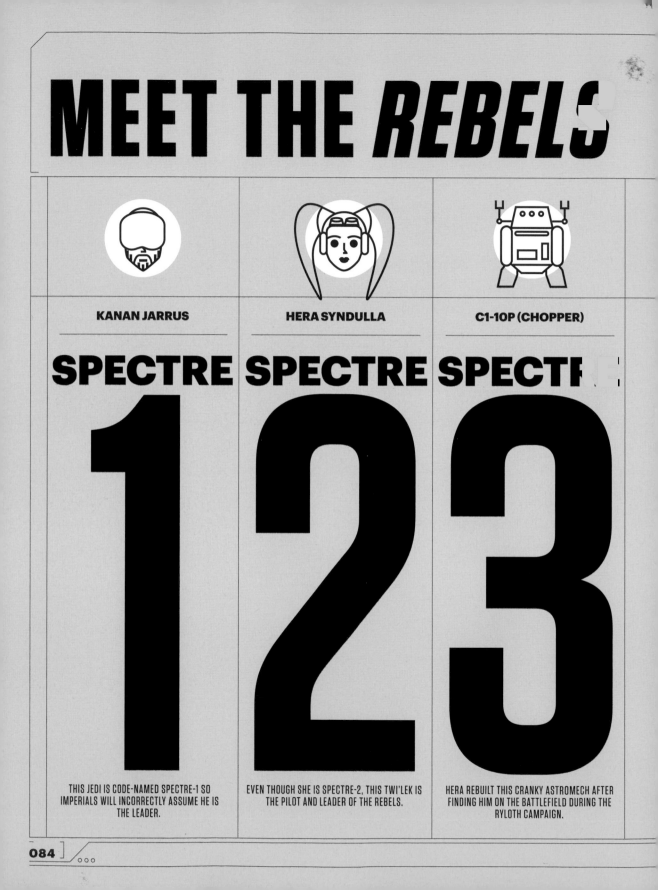

KANAN JARRUS

SPECTRE 1

THIS JEDI IS CODE-NAMED SPECTRE-1 SO IMPERIALS WILL INCORRECTLY ASSUME HE IS THE LEADER.

HERA SYNDULLA

SPECTRE 2

EVEN THOUGH SHE IS SPECTRE-2, THIS TWI'LEK IS THE PILOT AND LEADER OF THE REBELS.

C1-10P (CHOPPER)

SPECTRE 3

HERA REBUILT THIS CRANKY ASTROMECH AFTER FINDING HIM ON THE BATTLEFIELD DURING THE RYLOTH CAMPAIGN.

Code names for the crew of the *Ghost* in *Star Wars Rebels*.

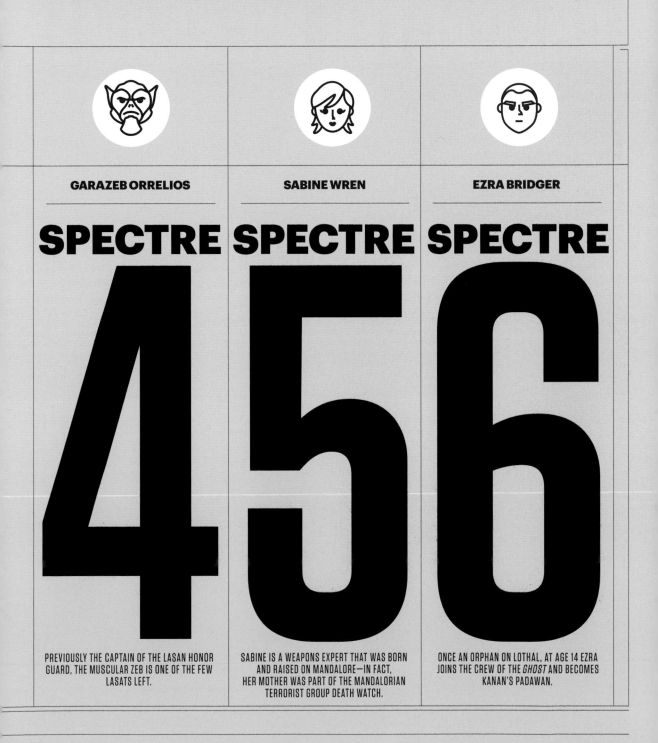

GARAZEB ORRELIOS

SPECTRE

4

PREVIOUSLY THE CAPTAIN OF THE LASAN HONOR GUARD, THE MUSCULAR ZEB IS ONE OF THE FEW LASATS LEFT.

SABINE WREN

SPECTRE

5

SABINE IS A WEAPONS EXPERT THAT WAS BORN AND RAISED ON MANDALORE—IN FACT, HER MOTHER WAS PART OF THE MANDALORIAN TERRORIST GROUP DEATH WATCH.

EZRA BRIDGER

SPECTRE

6

ONCE AN ORPHAN ON LOTHAL, AT AGE 14 EZRA JOINS THE CREW OF THE *GHOST* AND BECOMES KANAN'S PADAWAN.

CHARACTER NICKNAMES

Whether they're affectionate or degrading, these sobriquets add to the story's playfulness.

GRAMPS
(MASTER SINUUBE)

GRAMPS
(ANAKIN)

AGEIST

KID
(LUKE)

HUTTSLAYER
(LEIA)

AFFECTIONATE

SKYGUY
(ANAKIN)

RIFF ON NAME

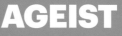

OBI
(OBI-WAN KENOBI)

REXTER
(CAPTAIN REX)

AGGIE
(AGGADEENN)

ARTOOIE
(R2-D2)

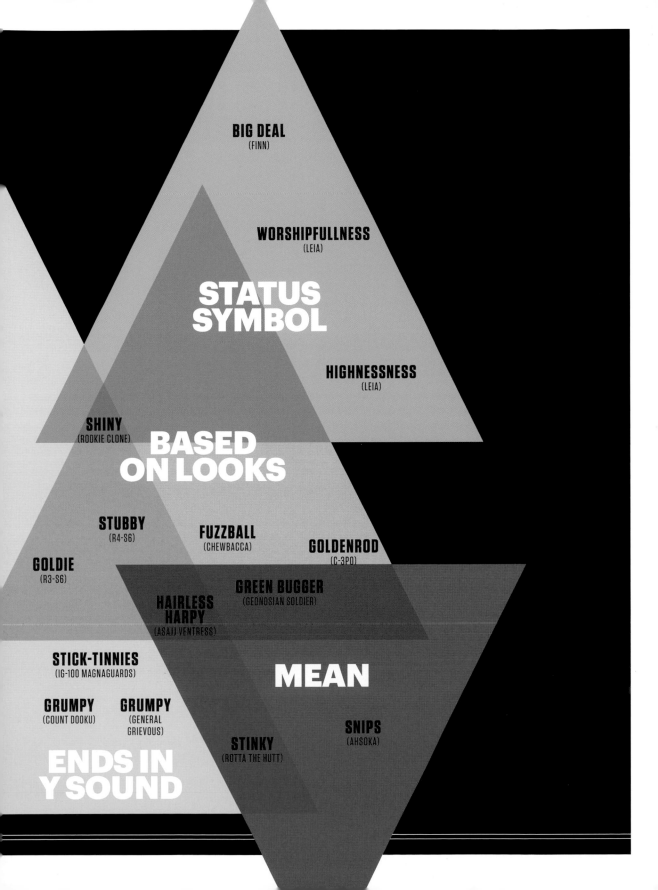

INSULTS BY THE NUMBERS

LAME		REAL ZINGER

LEIA

"ABSOLUTELY YOUR WORSHIP." —**HAN SOLO**

"LOOK … YOUR WORSHIPFULNESS." —**HAN SOLO**

"YOU REBEL SCUM" —**IMPERIAL OFFICER**

"YOU ARE PART OF THE REBEL ALLIANCE AND A TRAITOR!" —**DARTH VADER**

MILLENNIUM FALCON

"THIS BUCKET OF BOLTS'S NEVER GONNA GET US PAST THAT BLOCKADE." —**LEIA ORGANA**

"THAT ONE'S GARBAGE!" —**REY**

"WHAT A PIECE OF JUNK!" —**LUKE SKYWALKER**

"YOU CAME IN THAT THING? YOU'RE BRAVER THAN I THOUGHT. —**LEIA ORGANA**

R2-D2

"NO, I DON'T THINK HE LIKES YOU AT ALL. AND I DON'T LIKE YOU EITHER." —**C-3PO**

"YOU'LL BE MALFUNCTIONING WITHIN A DAY, YOU NEAR-SIGHTED SCRAP PILE." —**C-3PO**

"DON'T CALL ME A MINDLESS PHILOSOPHER, YOU OVERWEIGHT GLOB OF GREASE." —**C-3PO**

"STUPID LITTLE SHORT-CIRCUIT!" —**C-3PO**

These six characters received more verbal barbs than any other. Here's how much they stung—and who slung them.

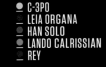

- C-3PO
- LEIA ORGANA
- HAN SOLO
- LANDO CALRISSIAN
- REY
- DARTH VADER
- IMPERIAL OFFICER
- LUKE SKYWALKER
- OWEN LARS

LAME · REAL ZINGER

HAN SOLO

"YOU STUCK-UP, HALF-WITTED, SCRUFFY-LOOKING NERF HERDER!" —LEIA ORGANA

"I DON'T KNOW WHERE YOU GET YOUR DELUSIONS LASER BRAIN." —LEIA ORGANA

"WHY, YOU SLIMY, DOUBLE-CROSSING, NO-GOOD SWINDLER." —LANDO CALRISSIAN

HAN: "I'M TRYING TO BE HELPFUL." LEIA: "WHEN DID THAT EVER HELP?"

OBI-WAN KENOBI

"YOUR POWERS ARE WEAK, OLD MAN." —DARTH VADER

"DAMN FOOL, I KNEW YOU WERE GOING TO SAY THAT." —HAN SOLO

"WHERE DID YOU DIG UP THAT OLD FOSSIL?" —HAN SOLO

"THAT WIZARD'S JUST A CRAZY OLD MAN." —OWEN LARS

CHEWBACCA

"I THOUGHT THAT HAIRY BEAST WOULD BE THE END OF ME." —C-3PO

"WILL SOMEBODY GET THIS BIG WALKING CARPET OUT OF MY WAY?" —LEIA ORGANA

"GET IN THERE YOU BIG, FURRY OAF!" —HAN SOLO

"LAUGH IT UP, FUZZBALL" —HAN SOLO

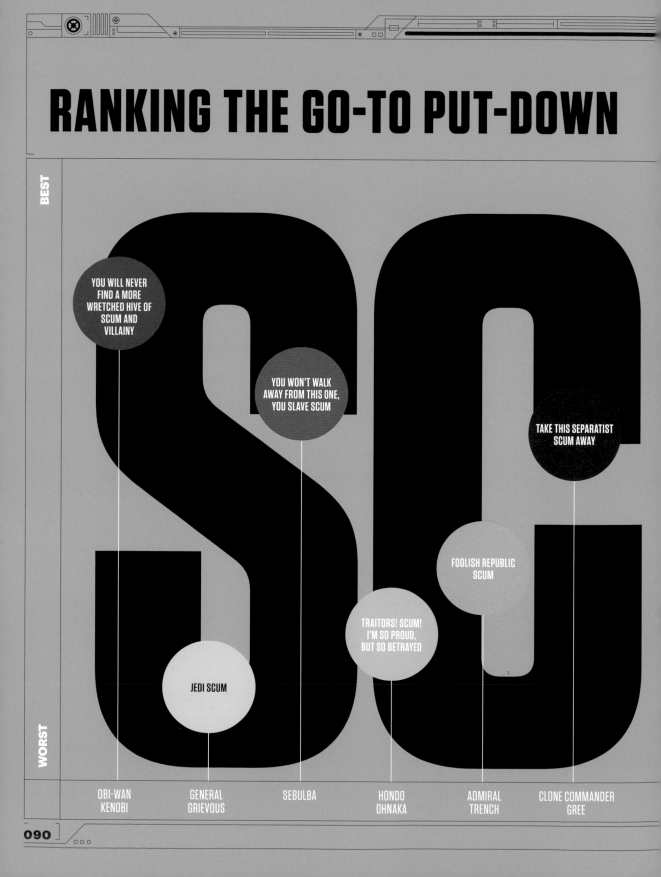

BEST

WORST

YOU WILL NEVER FIND A MORE WRETCHED HIVE OF SCUM AND VILLAINY

YOU WON'T WALK AWAY FROM THIS ONE, YOU SLAVE SCUM

TAKE THIS SEPARATIST SCUM AWAY

FOOLISH REPUBLIC SCUM

TRAITORS! SCUM! I'M SO PROUD, BUT SO BETRAYED

JEDI SCUM

OBI-WAN KENOBI

GENERAL GRIEVOUS

SEBULBA

HONDO OHNAKA

ADMIRAL TRENCH

CLONE COMMANDER GREE

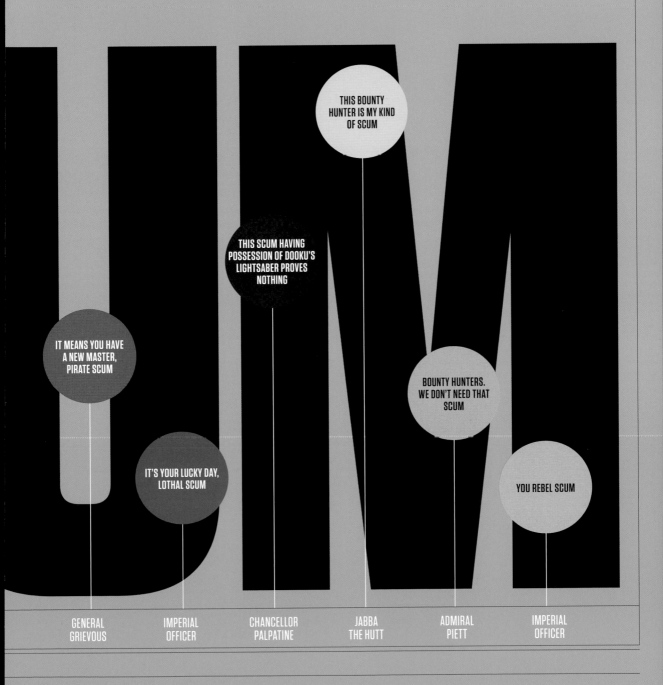

THIS BOUNTY HUNTER IS MY KIND OF SCUM

THIS SCUM HAVING POSSESSION OF DOOKU'S LIGHTSABER PROVES NOTHING

IT MEANS YOU HAVE A NEW MASTER, PIRATE SCUM

BOUNTY HUNTERS. WE DON'T NEED THAT SCUM

IT'S YOUR LUCKY DAY, LOTHAL SCUM

YOU REBEL SCUM

GENERAL GRIEVOUS

IMPERIAL OFFICER

CHANCELLOR PALPATINE

JABBA THE HUTT

ADMIRAL PIETT

IMPERIAL OFFICER

VILLAINY IN JABBA'S PALACE

THE RANCOR
BOBA FETT
SALACIOUS B. CRUMB
GAMORREAN GUARD
BIB FORTUNA

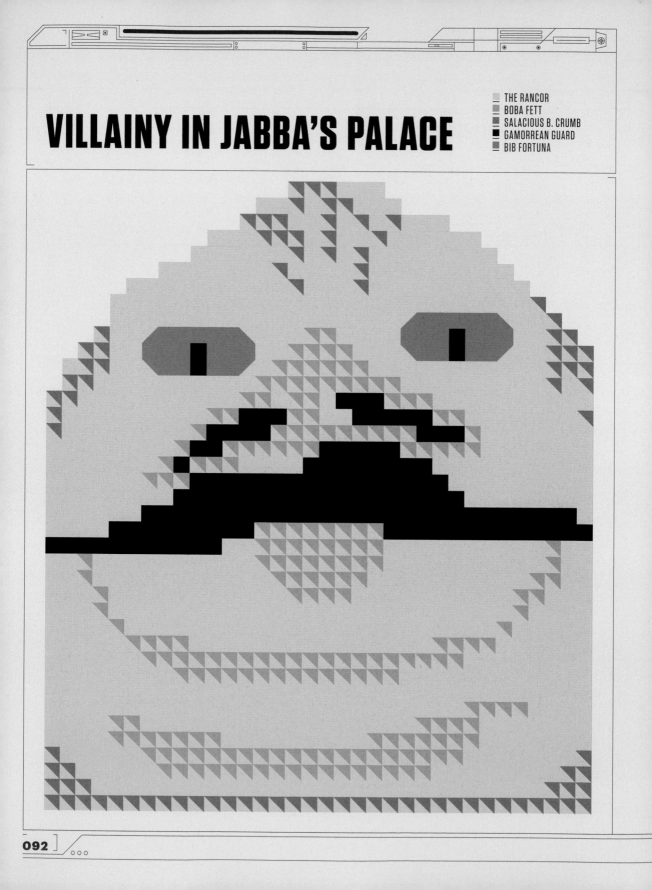

THE JAWAS'S WARES

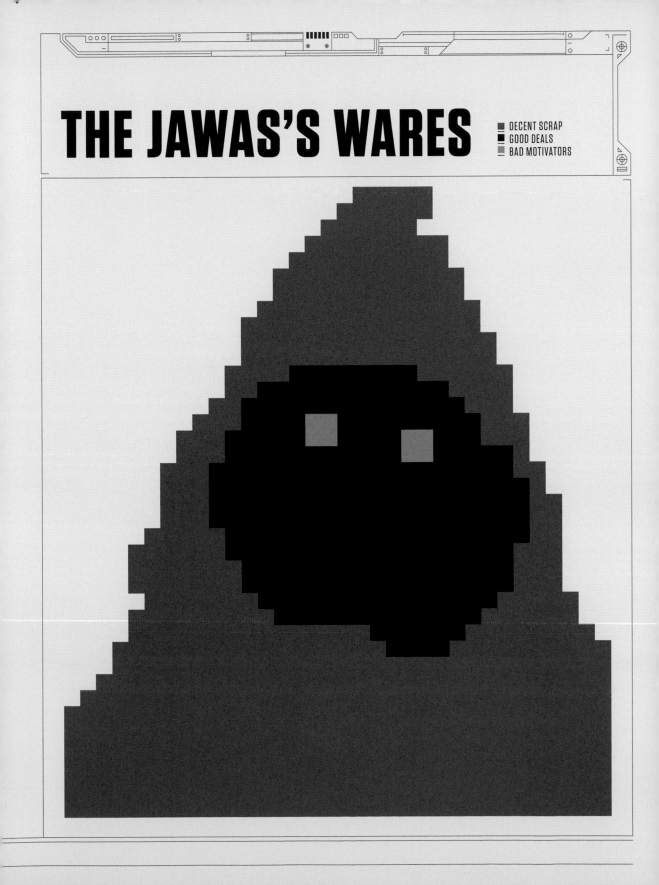

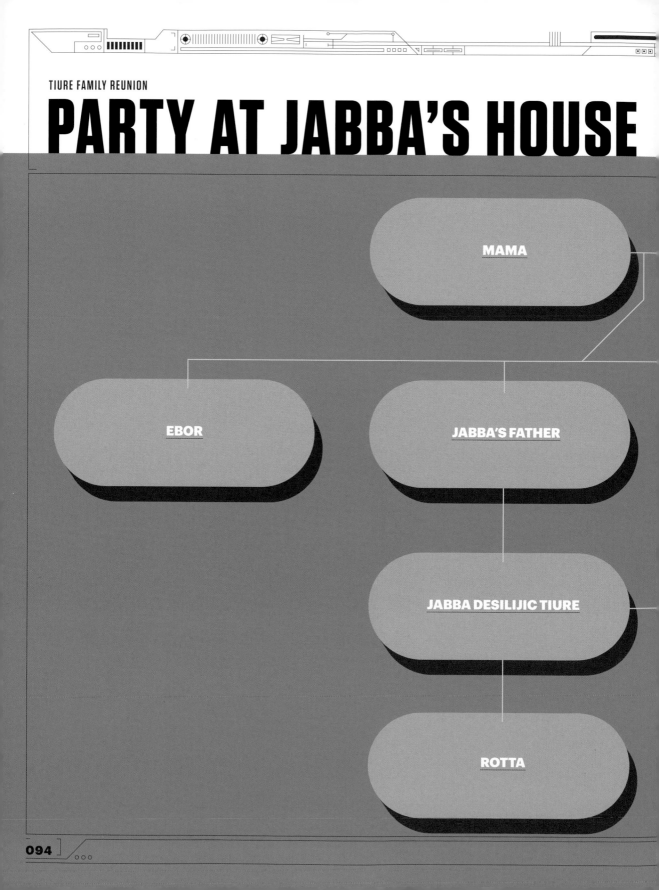

PARTY AT JABBA'S HOUSE

MAMA

EBOR

JABBA'S FATHER

JABBA DESILIJIC TIURE

ROTTA

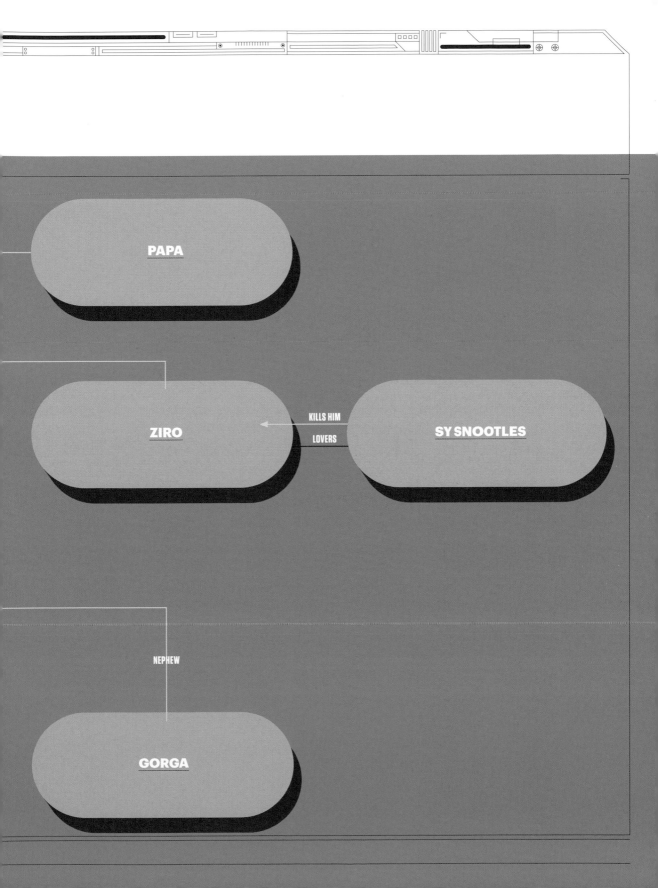

SLOW FOOD MOVEMENT

A timeline of Sarlacc digestion.

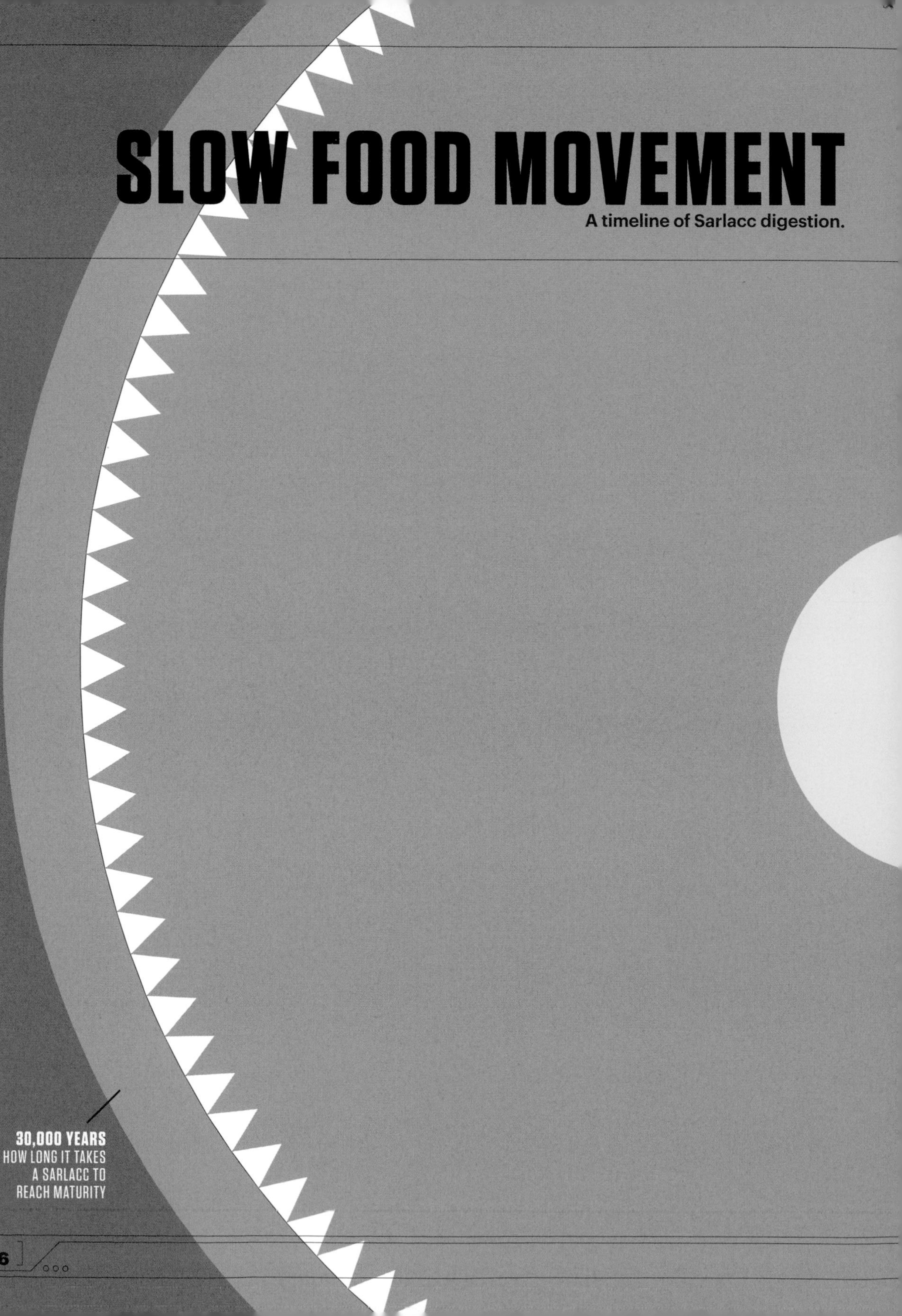

30,000 YEARS
HOW LONG IT TAKES
A SARLACC TO
REACH MATURITY

"IN ITS BELLY, YOU WILL FIND A NEW DEFINITION OF PAIN AND SUFFERING AS YOU ARE SLOWLY DIGESTED OVER A ... THOUSAND YEARS."
—C-3PO, TRANSLATING FOR JABBA THE HUTT

That sounds like a long time ... until you realize how long it takes the Sarlacc to grow up.

1,000 YEARS
HOW LONG IT TAKES
A SARLACC TO DIGEST
YOU (WHILE YOU'RE
STILL ALIVE ... GULP)

WITH A LITTLE HELP FROM MY FRIENDS

It's a dangerous universe out there. Big risks don't always succeed. But when characters find themselves in a tight spot these people (or groups) swoop in to save them (or at least try to).

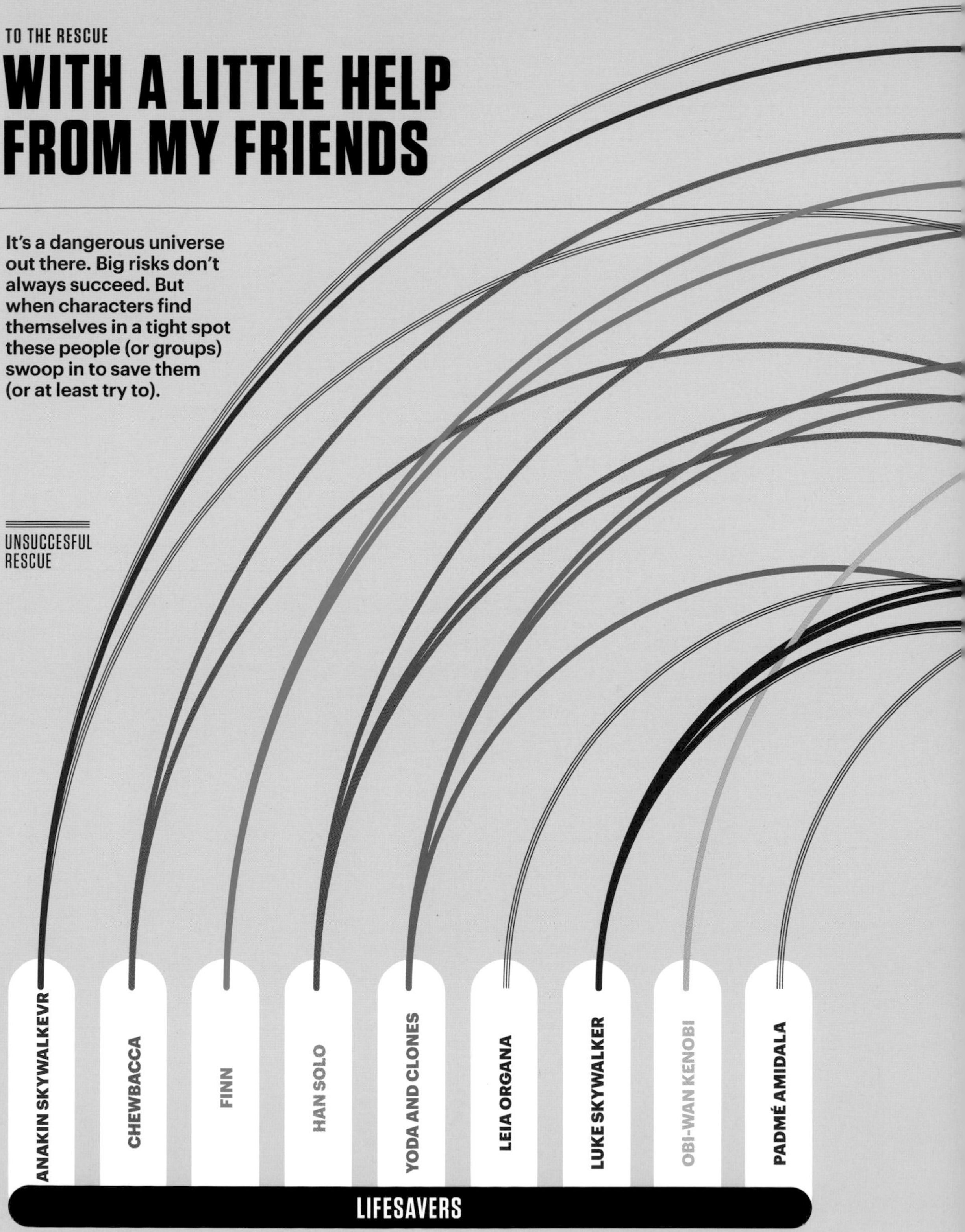

UNSUCCESFUL
RESCUE

ANAKIN SKYWALKEVR

CHEWBACCA

FINN

HAN SOLO

YODA AND CLONES

LEIA ORGANA

LUKE SKYWALKER

OBI-WAN KENOBI

PADMÉ AMIDALA

LIFESAVERS

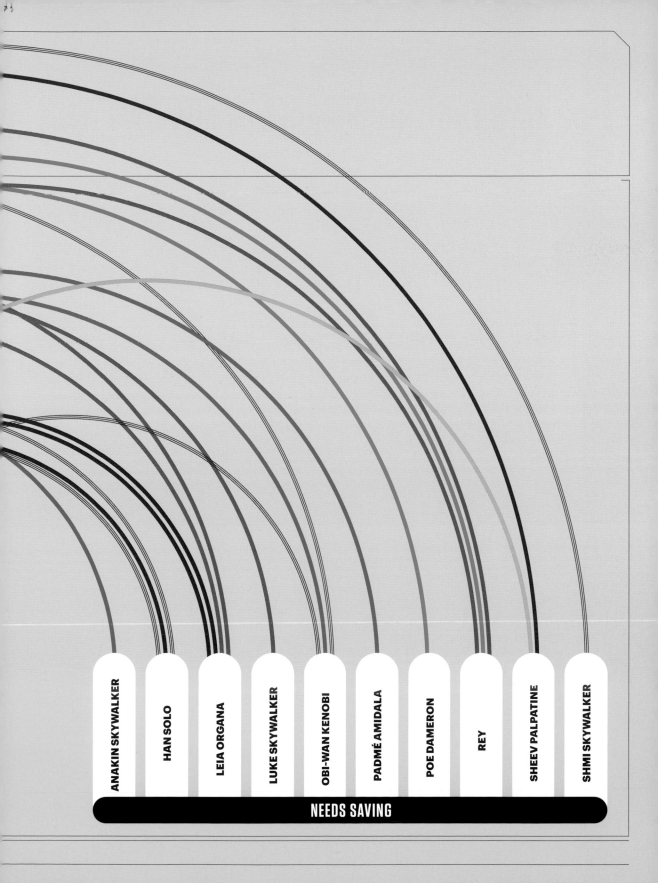

ANAKIN SKYWALKER

HAN SOLO

LEIA ORGANA

LUKE SKYWALKER

OBI-WAN KENOBI

PADMÉ AMIDALA

POE DAMERON

REY

SHEEV PALPATINE

SHMI SKYWALKER

NEEDS SAVING

After Luke is stranded in Hoth's freezing weather in *The Empire Strikes Back* ...

R2-D2 SAYS THAT THE CHANCES OF SURVIVAL ARE

725 | ▪ 1

725 to 1

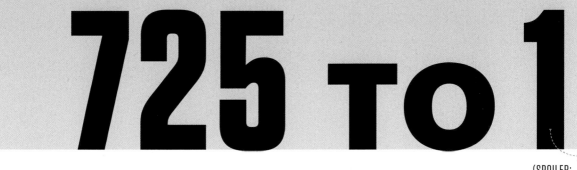

(SPOILER:
LUKE
SURVIVES)

PADMĒ AMIDALA

OBI-WAN KENOBI ——— SATINE KRYZE

CIENA REE ——— THANE KYRELL

QUINLAN VOS ———

SHMI SKYWALKER ——— CLIEGG LARS

LEIA ORGANA ——— HAN SOLO

BAIL ORGANA ——— BREHA ORGANA

KANAN JARRUS ——— HERA SYNDULLA

BERU LARS ——— OWEN LARS

SHARA BEY ——— KES DAMERON

LIGHT SIDE

ANAKIN SKYWALKER

SY SNOOTLES ———————————— ZIRO THE HUTT

ASAJJ VENTRESS

STAR-CROSSED LOVERS

FROM NABOO, WITH LOVE

Ranking romantic pairs.

EVERY TRANSITION WIPE

WIPES PER MOVIE

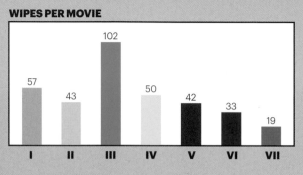

I	II	III	IV	V	VI	VII
57	43	102	50	42	33	19

SIDE TO SIDE

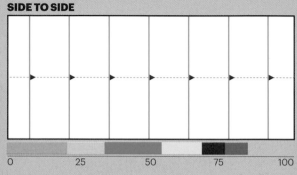

0 25 50 75 100

SCREEN SPLIT RADIAL

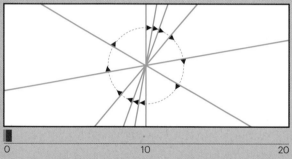

0 10 20

DIAGONAL CORNER TO CORNER

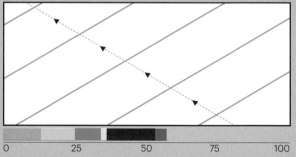

0 25 50 75 100

ELEVATOR DOORS (HORIZONTAL AND VERTICAL)

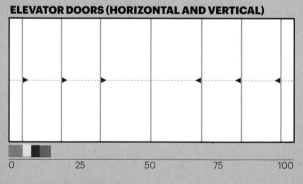

0 25 50 75 100

UP AND DOWN

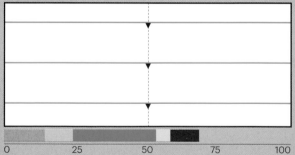

0 25 50 75 100

EXPANDING SHAPES

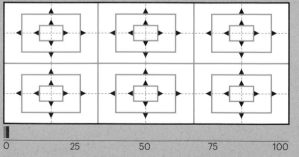

0 25 50 75 100

5-SPLIT TOP TO BOTTOM

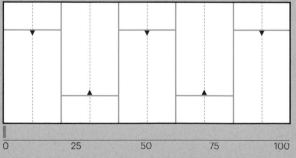

0 25 50 75 100

Star Wars is famous for its many visual cues, but one often overlooked gem is its transition wipes between scenes. Here's a breakdown of which kinds were used, and how often.

WINDSHIELD WIPER

| 0 | 25 | 50 | 75 | 100 |

360-DEGREE RADIAL

| 0 | 25 | 50 | 75 | 100 |

SHRINKING/EXPANDING CIRCLE

| 0 | 25 | 50 | 75 | 100 |

MURKY FADE

| 0 | 25 | 50 | 75 | 100 |

DIAGONAL SPLIT TO CORNERS

| 0 | 25 | 50 | 75 | 100 |

5-POINT SIDE TO SIDE

| 0 | 25 | 50 | 75 | 100 |

CLOSING BOOK TO CENTER

| 0 | 25 | 50 | 75 | 100 |

SPLIT TOP TO BOTTOM

| 0 | 25 | 50 | 75 | 100 |

K-2SO'S ASSESSMENT

K-2SO's odds of Jyn using her blaster on Cassian.

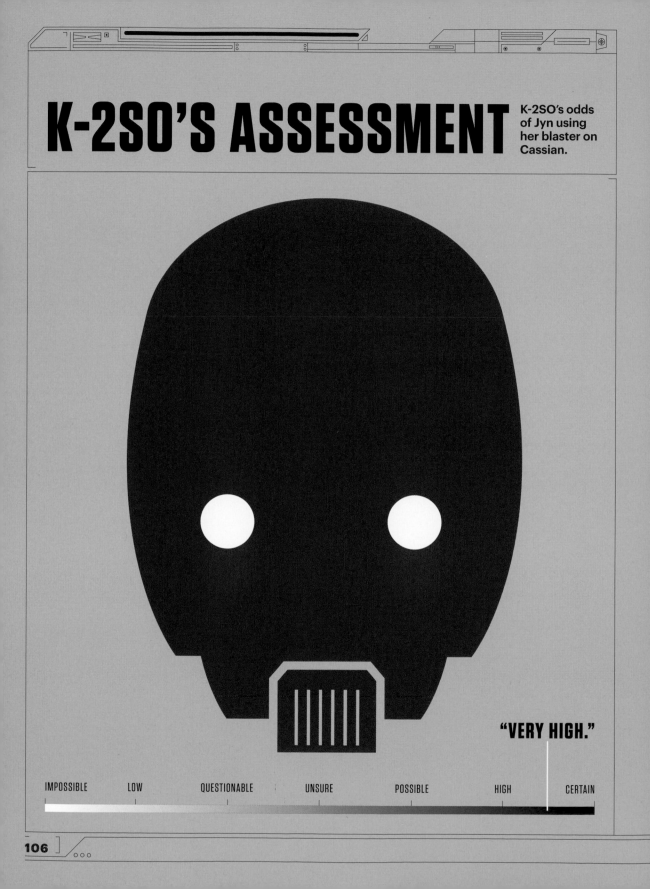

"VERY HIGH."

| IMPOSSIBLE | LOW | QUESTIONABLE | UNSURE | POSSIBLE | HIGH | CERTAIN |

THE JEDI LEGEND

According to Han Solo.

○ TRUE. ALL OF IT.
● NOT TRUE.

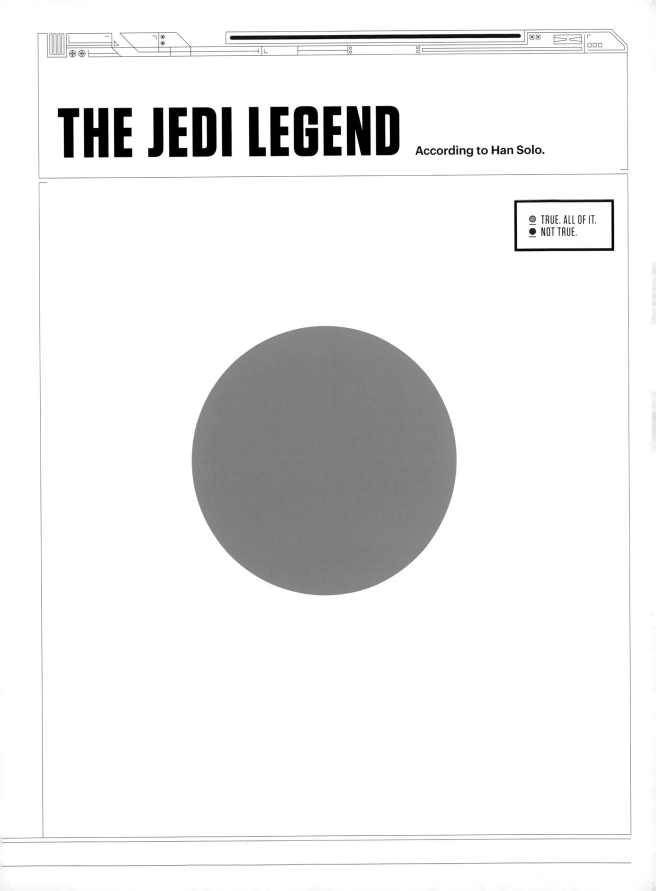

FINN
FATHER: UNKNOWN
TAKEN FROM HIS PARENTS BY THE
FIRST ORDER AS A CHILD.

REY
FATHER: UNKNOWN
HER FAMILY LEFT HER ON JAKKU
AS A CHILD.

JYN ERSO
FATHER: GALEN ERSO
HER MOTHER WAS KILLED
AND HER FATHER WAS CAPTURED
WHEN SHE WAS NINE.

SEPARATED FROM PARENTS

ANAKIN SKYWALKER
FATHER: UNKNOWN
HE NEVER KNEW ANYTHING
ABOUT HIS FATHER.

EZRA BRIDGER
FATHER: EPHRAIM BRIDGER
THE EMPIRE TOOK HIS PARENTS WHEN HE WAS SEVEN.

A VENN DIAGRAM OF DADDY ISSUES

With shifting allegiances, disappearances, and sometimes tragedy, fatherhood in *Star Wars* is complicated.

HERA SYNDULLA
FATHER: CHAM SYNDULLA
AFTER HER MOTHER'S DEATH, HER FATHER PUTS THE RYLOTH REBELLION BEFORE HIS FAMILY.

DIVIDED BY FUNDAMENTAL DISAGREEMENTS

LUKE SKYWALKER
FATHER: ANAKIN SKYWALKER
HIDDEN FROM HIS FATHER AS A BABY, LUKE BECOMES A JEDI AND FIGHTS HIS SITH-FATHER. AS HIS FATHER SUCCUMBS TO INJURIES, LUKE HOLDS HIM.

KYLO REN
FATHER: HAN SOLO
KILLED HIS FATHER

LEIA ORGANA
FATHER: ANAKIN SKYWALKER
ADOPTIVE FATHER: BAIL ORGANA
LEADS A REBELLION AGAINST HER FATHER. THEN WATCHES AS HIS BOSS DESTROYS HER ADOPTIVE PARENTS (AND THE REST OF ALDERAAN).

WITNESSED FATHER'S DEATH

BOBA FETT
FATHER: JANGO FETT
FATHER WAS DECAPITATED BY MACE WINDU NOT FAR FROM HIM.

IS AN EXACT CLONE OF FATHER

THE RESULT OF EVERY DUEL

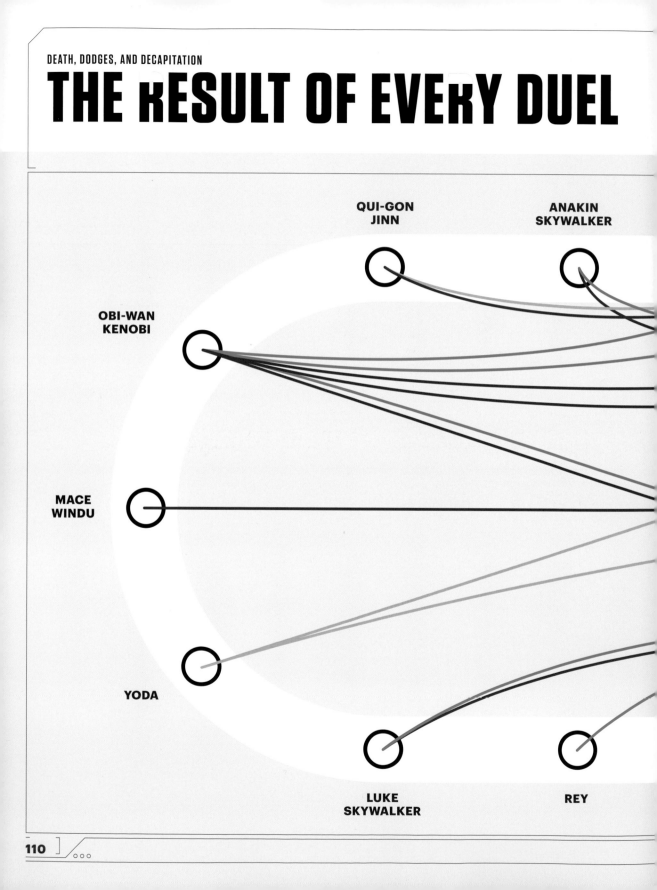

QUI-GON
JINN

ANAKIN
SKYWALKER

OBI-WAN
KENOBI

MACE
WINDU

YODA

LUKE
SKYWALKER

REY

The outcome of every
lightsaber duel shown
in the films.

WINS
- LIGHT SIDE
- DARK SIDE
- DRAW

NUMBER OF OVERALL DUELS WON

8
6
3

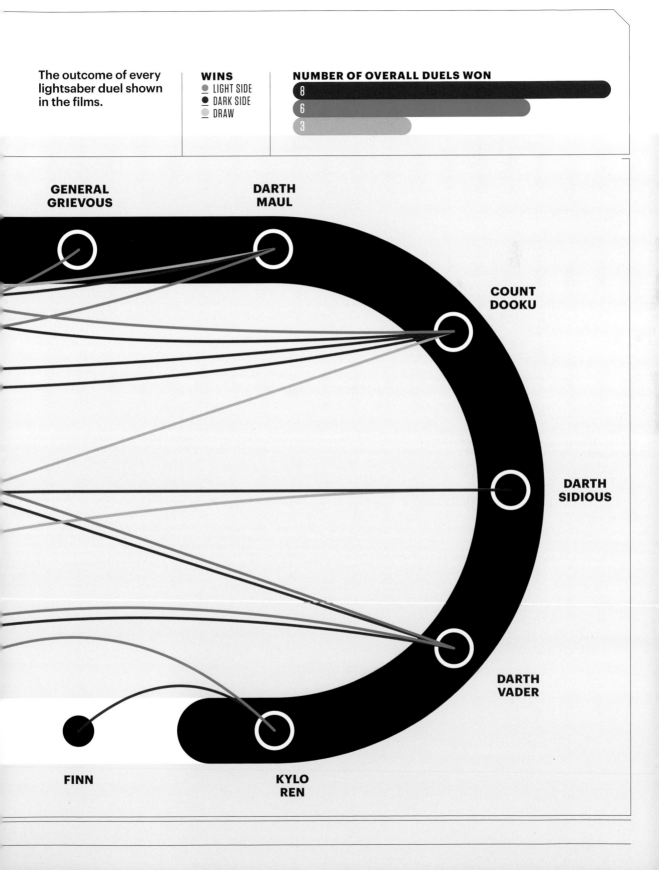

GENERAL
GRIEVOUS

DARTH
MAUL

COUNT
DOOKU

DARTH
SIDIOUS

DARTH
VADER

FINN

KYLO
REN

LIFE AND DEATH SITUATIONS

When your favorite characters overlapped in time.

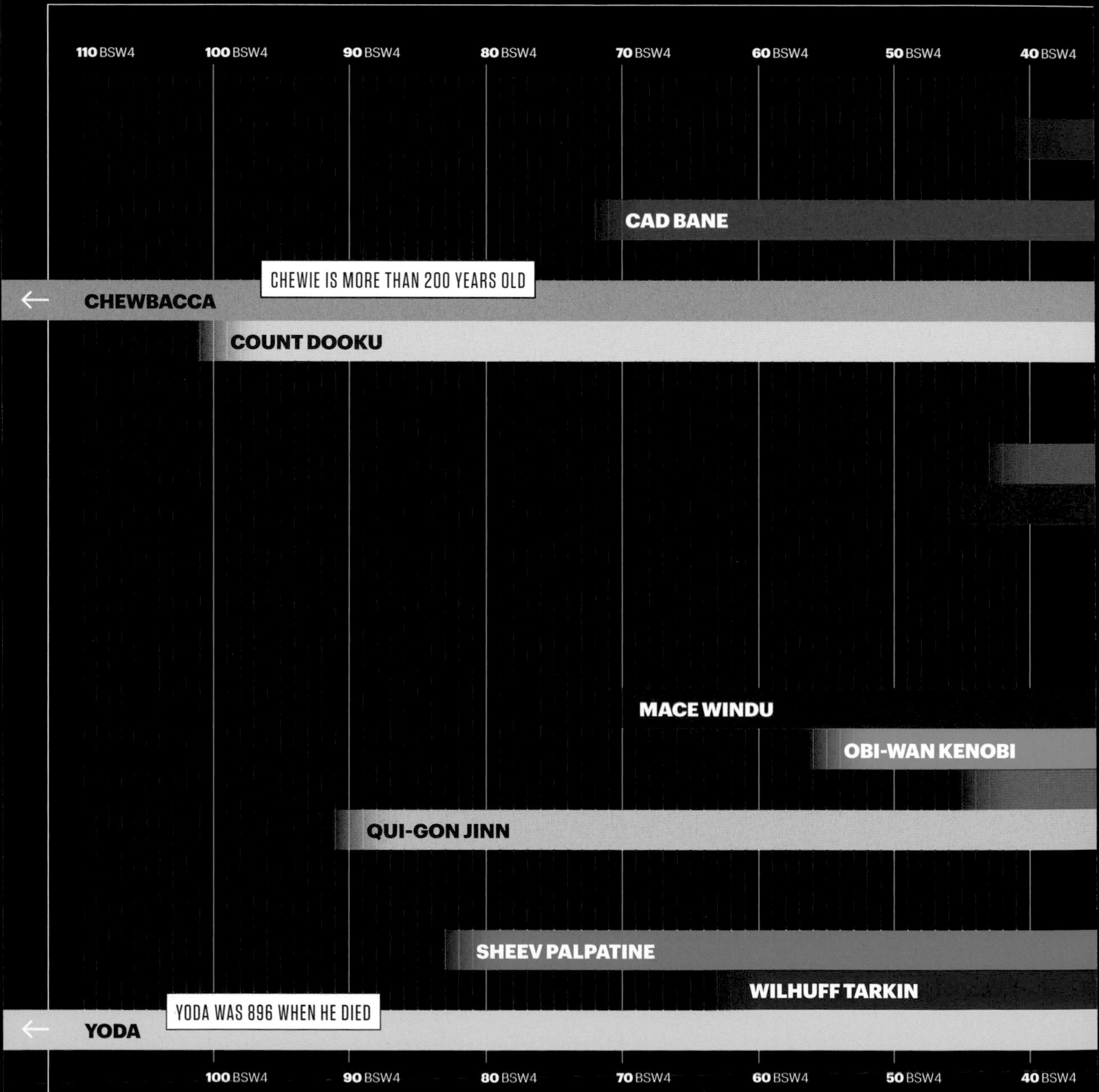

| 110 BSW4 | 100 BSW4 | 90 BSW4 | 80 BSW4 | 70 BSW4 | 60 BSW4 | 50 BSW4 | 40 BSW4 |

CAD BANE

← **CHEWBACCA** CHEWIE IS MORE THAN 200 YEARS OLD

COUNT DOOKU

MACE WINDU

OBI-WAN KENOBI

QUI-GON JINN

SHEEV PALPATINE

WILHUFF TARKIN

YODA WAS 896 WHEN HE DIED

← **YODA**

| 100 BSW4 | 90 BSW4 | 80 BSW4 | 70 BSW4 | 60 BSW4 | 50 BSW4 | 40 BSW4 |

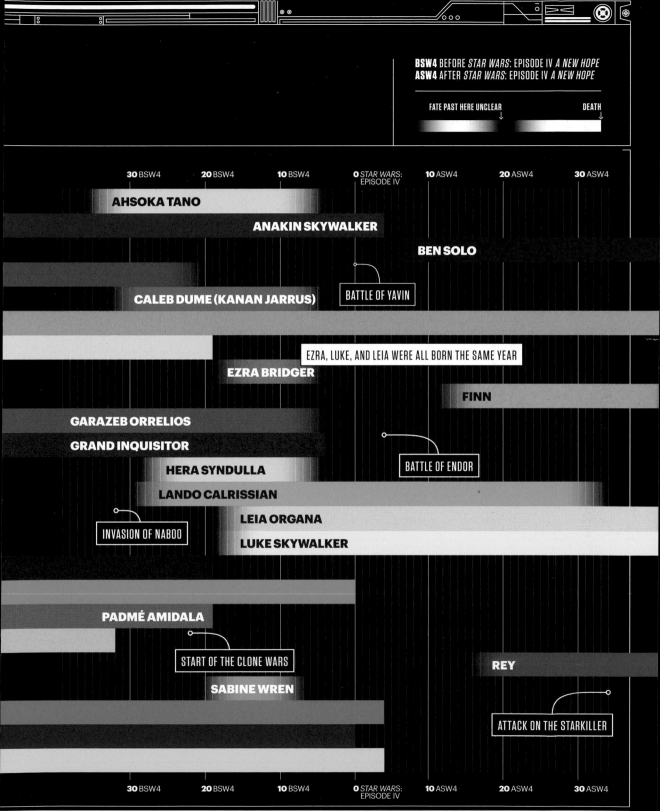

30 BSW4 **20** BSW4 **10** BSW4 **0** *STAR WARS*: EPISODE IV **10** ASW4 **20** ASW4 **30** ASW4

AHSOKA TANO

ANAKIN SKYWALKER

BEN SOLO

BATTLE OF YAVIN

CALEB DUME (KANAN JARRUS)

EZRA, LUKE, AND LEIA WERE ALL BORN THE SAME YEAR

EZRA BRIDGER

FINN

GARAZEB ORRELIOS

GRAND INQUISITOR

BATTLE OF ENDOR

HERA SYNDULLA

LANDO CALRISSIAN

LEIA ORGANA

INVASION OF NABOO

LUKE SKYWALKER

PADMÉ AMIDALA

START OF THE CLONE WARS

REY

SABINE WREN

ATTACK ON THE STARKILLER

30 BSW4 **20** BSW4 **10** BSW4 **0** *STAR WARS*: EPISODE IV **10** ASW4 **20** ASW4 **30** ASW4

BATTLE TESTED

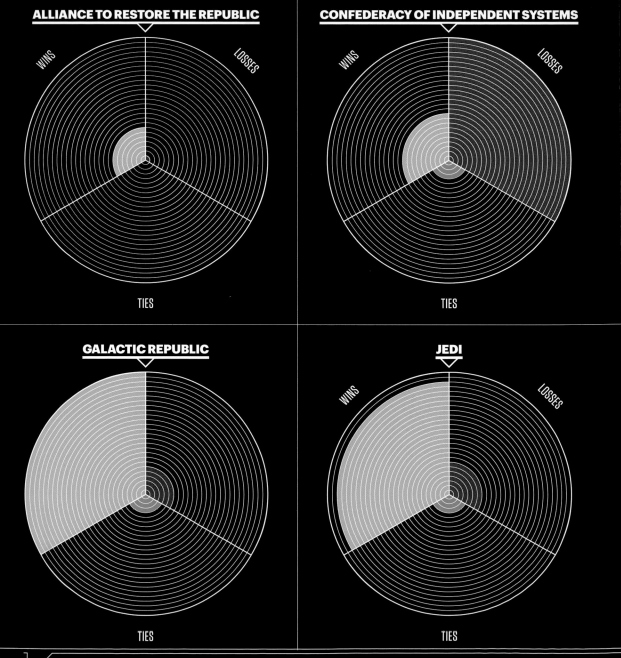

ALLIANCE TO RESTORE THE REPUBLIC

WINS

LOSSES

TIES

CONFEDERACY OF INDEPENDENT SYSTEMS

WINS

LOSSES

TIES

GALACTIC REPUBLIC

TIES

JEDI

WINS

LOSSES

TIES

How the competing factions
stack up in major battles (not duels)
in the films and TV series.

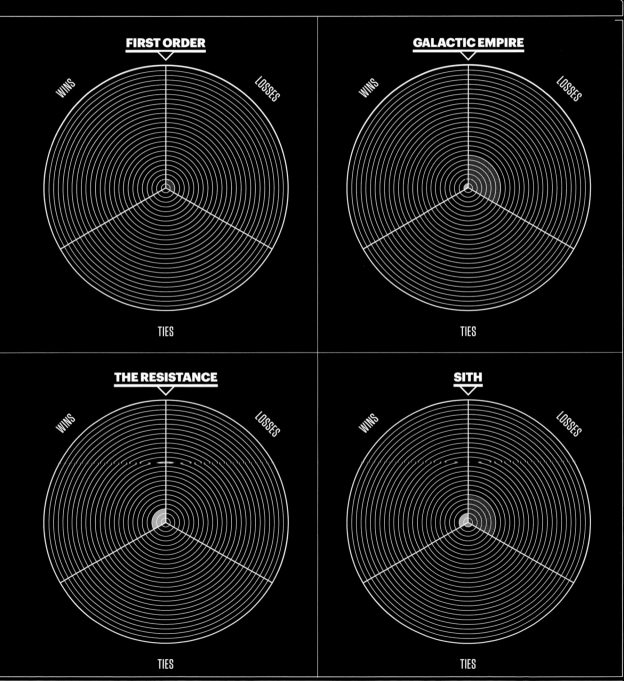

FIRST ORDER

WINS

LOSSES

TIES

GALACTIC EMPIRE

WINS

LOSSES

TIES

THE RESISTANCE

WINS

LOSSES

TIES

SITH

WINS

LOSSES

TIES

YODA

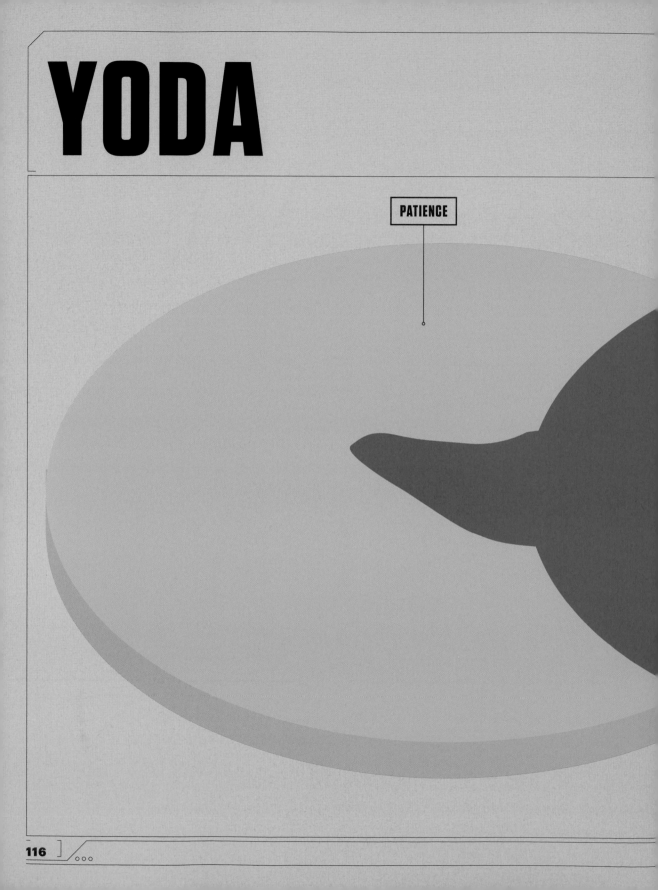

PATIENCE

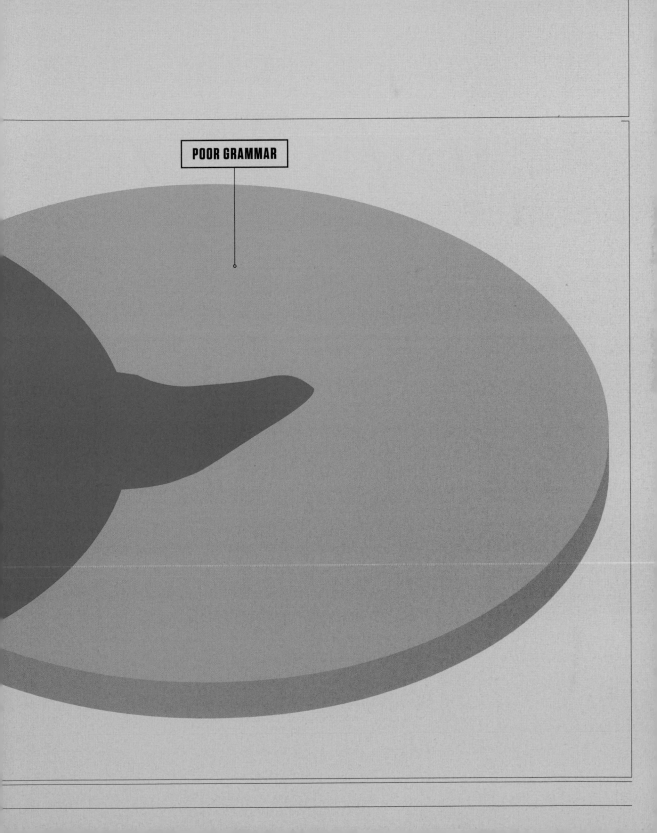

POOR GRAMMAR

The **REBELS**, the **RESISTANCE**, and the **JEDI**

ADMIRAL ACKBAR	LEIA ORGANA	HAN SOLO	C-3PO	CHEWBACCA	POE DAMERON	FINN	REY	PADMÉ AMIDALA

SPECTRUM)

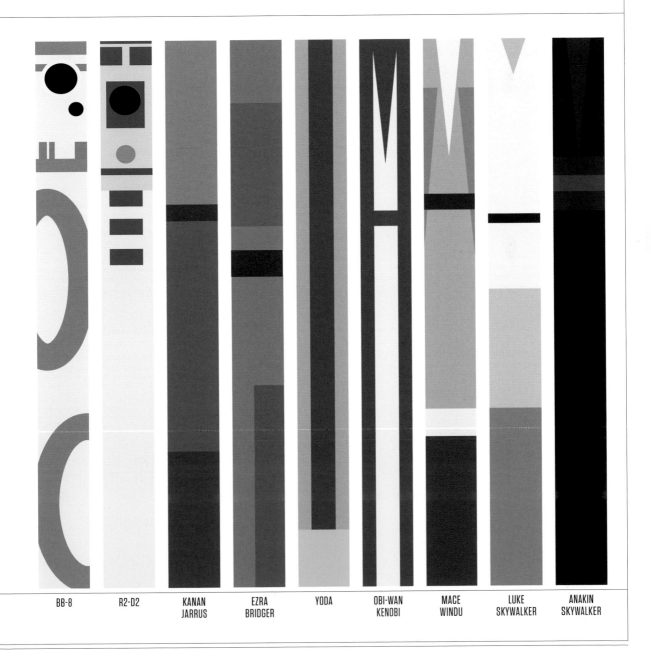

BB-8 · R2-D2 · KANAN JARRUS · EZRA BRIDGER · YODA · OBI-WAN KENOBI · MACE WINDU · LUKE SKYWALKER · ANAKIN SKYWALKER

THE DARK SIDE (OF THE COLOR

The EMPIRE, the FIRST ORDER, and the SITH

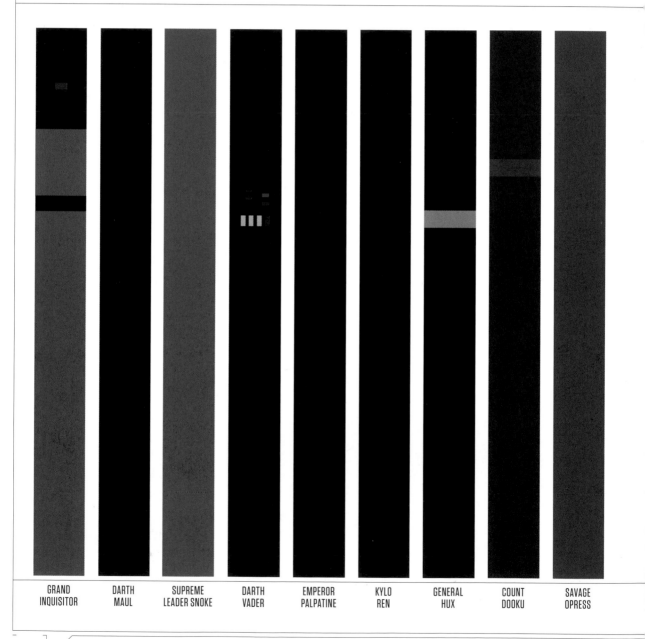

| GRAND INQUISITOR | DARTH MAUL | SUPREME LEADER SNOKE | DARTH VADER | EMPEROR PALPATINE | KYLO REN | GENERAL HUX | COUNT DOOKU | SAVAGE OPRESS |

SPECTRUM)

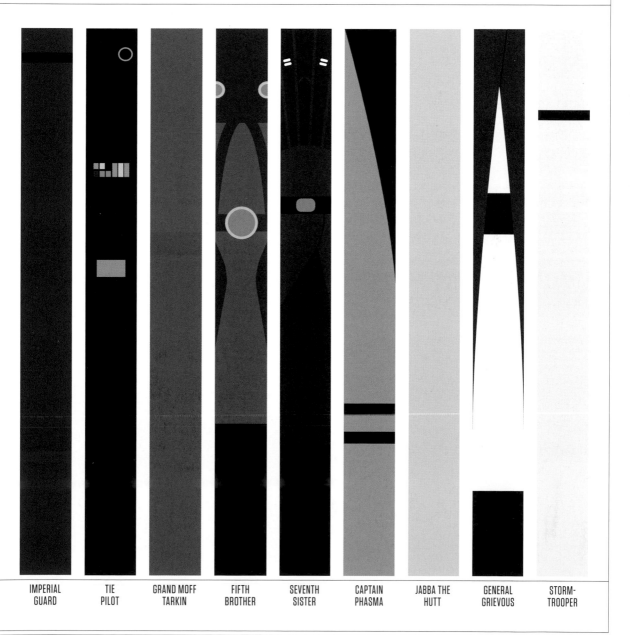

| IMPERIAL GUARD | TIE PILOT | GRAND MOFF TARKIN | FIFTH BROTHER | SEVENTH SISTER | CAPTAIN PHASMA | JABBA THE HUTT | GENERAL GRIEVOUS | STORM-TROOPER |

ROUTE TO THE DARK SIDE

"FEAR IS THE PATH TO THE DARK SIDE. FEAR LEADS TO ANGER. ANGER LEADS TO HATE. HATE LEADS TO SUFFERING" —YODA

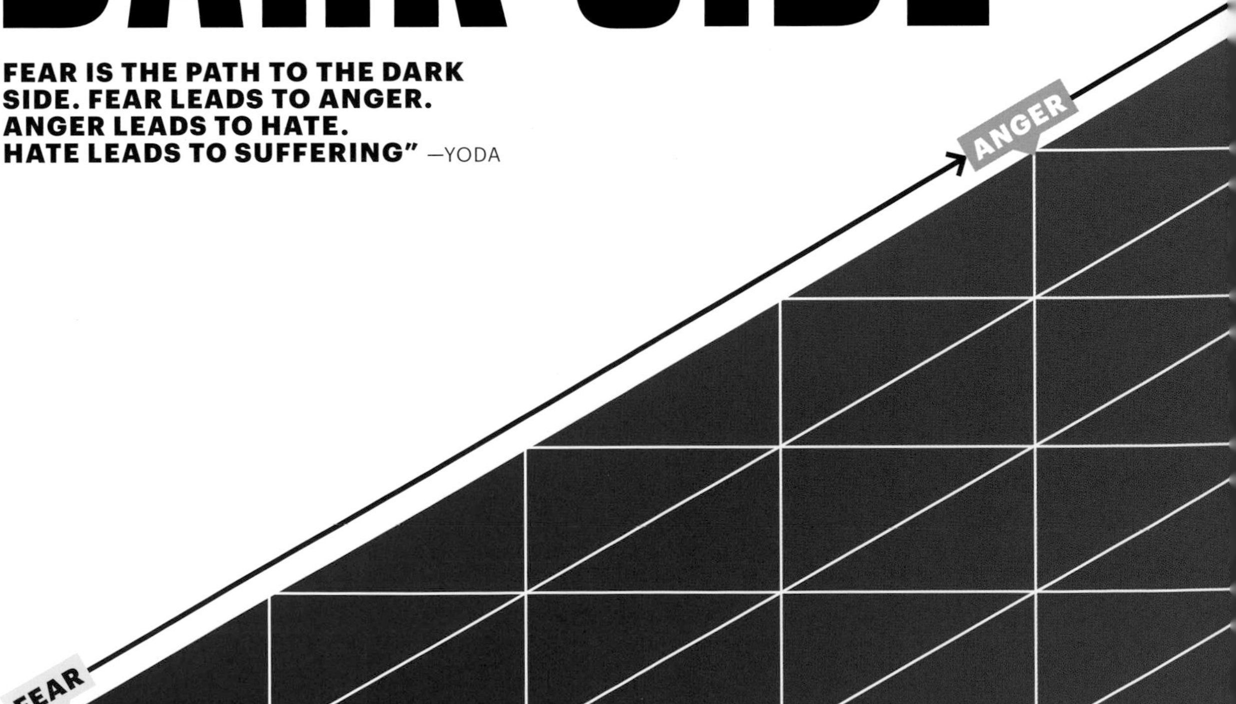

ANGER

FEAR

TIME

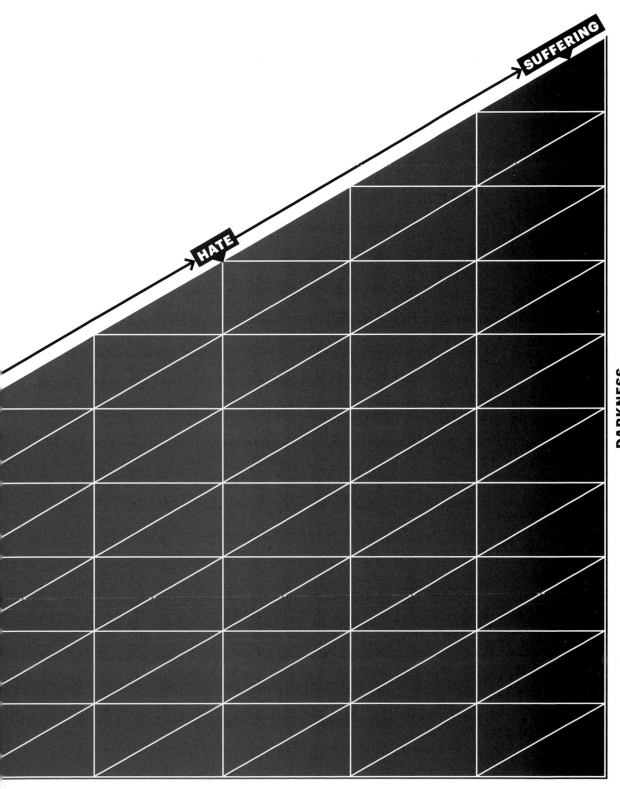

ORGANIZATIONAL STRUCTURE OF THE STORMTROOPER COMMAND

The Empire maintains control throughout the galaxy with a force that is built on the overwhelming number of troops.

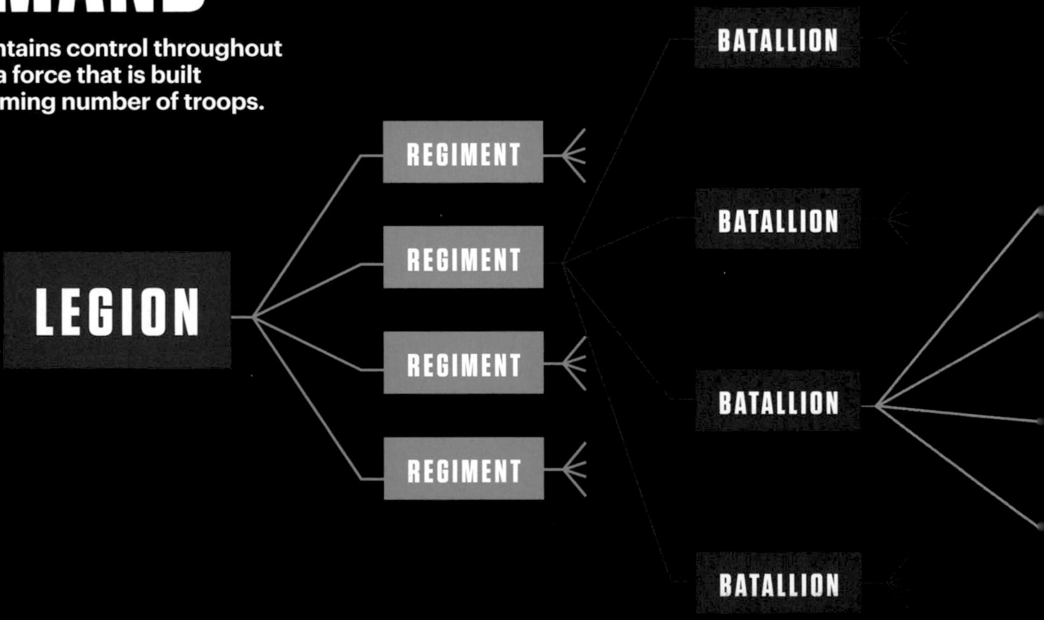

LEGION

REGIMENT

REGIMENT

REGIMENT

REGIMENT

BATALLION

BATALLION

BATALLION

BATALLION

BATALLION

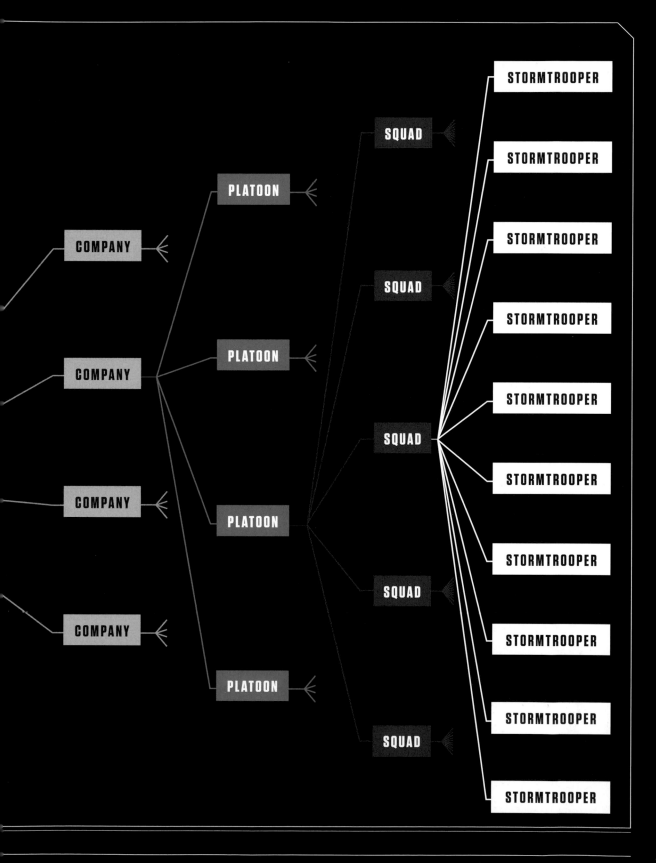

THAT'S NO MOON

Planet-destroying weapon size, by diameter.

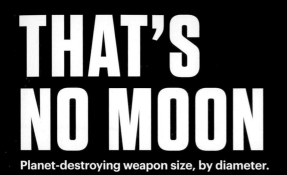

DEATH STAR
A NEW HOPE

For comparison, the *Millennium Falcon* is one-third the size of this green dot

STARKILLER BASE
THE FORCE AWAKENS

FOOL ME ONCE

These weapons of mass destruction have more than just a design flaw in common.

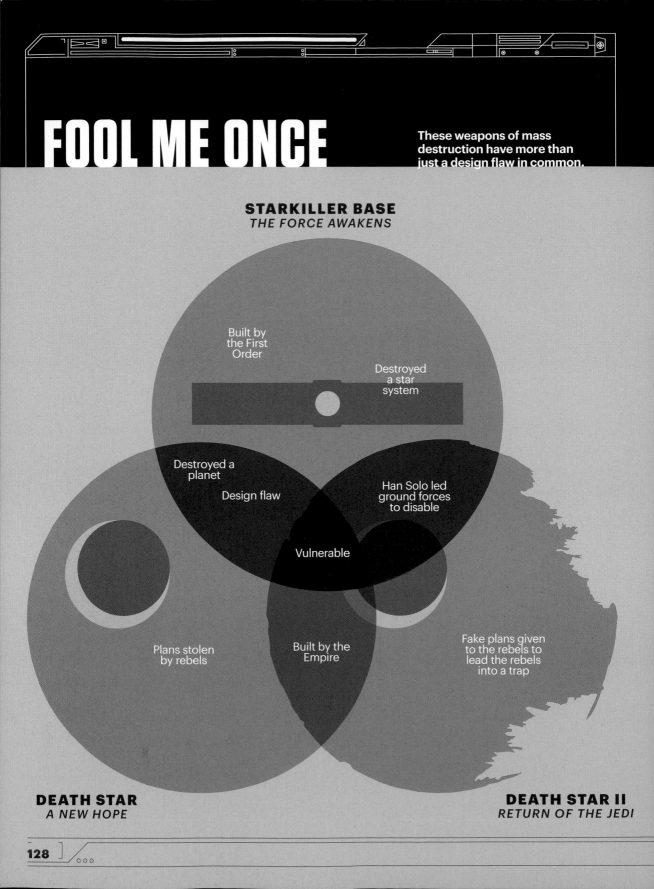

STARKILLER BASE
THE FORCE AWAKENS

Built by the First Order

Destroyed a star system

Destroyed a planet

Design flaw

Han Solo led ground forces to disable

Vulnerable

Plans stolen by rebels

Built by the Empire

Fake plans given to the rebels to lead the rebels into a trap

DEATH STAR
A NEW HOPE

DEATH STAR II
RETURN OF THE JEDI

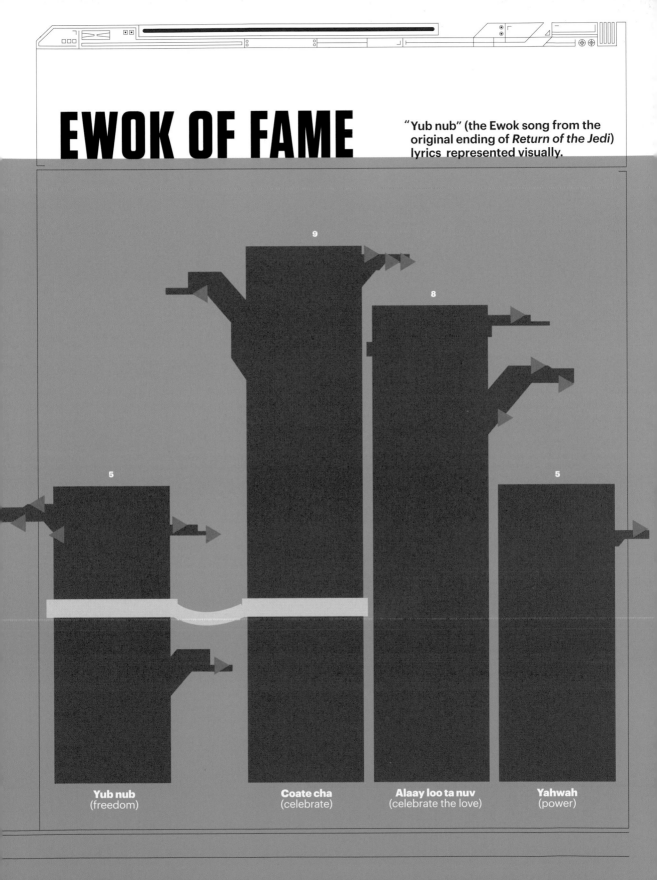

EWOK OF FAME

"Yub nub" (the Ewok song from the original ending of *Return of the Jedi*) lyrics represented visually.

Yub nub
(freedom)

Coate cha
(celebrate)

Alaay loo ta nuv
(celebrate the love)

Yahwah
(power)

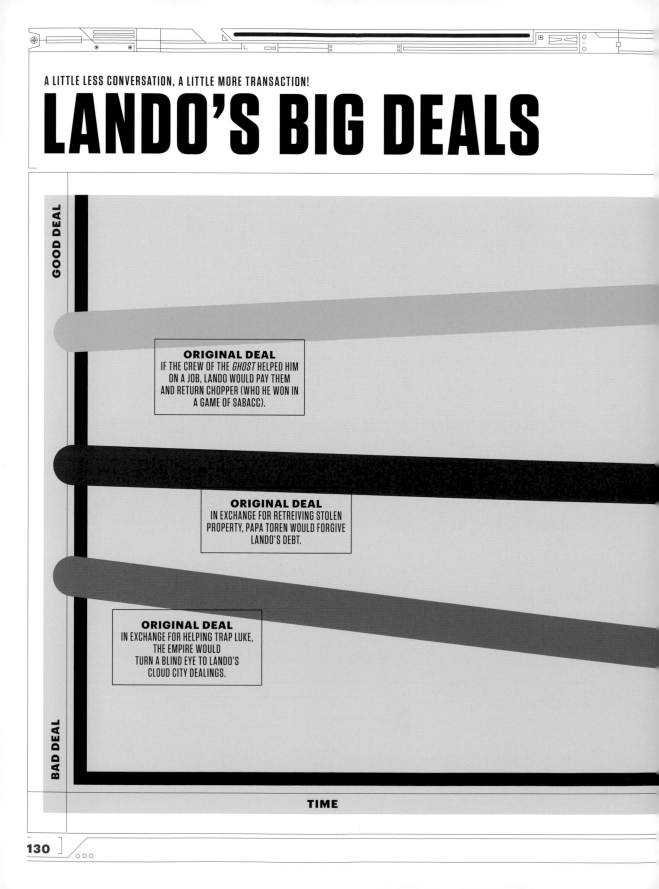

A LITTLE LESS CONVERSATION, A LITTLE MORE TRANSACTION!

LANDO'S BIG DEALS

GOOD DEAL

ORIGINAL DEAL
IF THE CREW OF THE *GHOST* HELPED HIM
ON A JOB, LANDO WOULD PAY THEM
AND RETURN CHOPPER (WHO HE WON IN
A GAME OF SABACC).

ORIGINAL DEAL
IN EXCHANGE FOR RETREIVING STOLEN
PROPERTY, PAPA TOREN WOULD FORGIVE
LANDO'S DEBT.

ORIGINAL DEAL
IN EXCHANGE FOR HELPING TRAP LUKE,
THE EMPIRE WOULD
TURN A BLIND EYE TO LANDO'S
CLOUD CITY DEALINGS.

BAD DEAL

TIME

The self-proclaimed businessman is no stranger to shady arrangements. Here's how this scoundrel's plans have worked out in the films, comics, and TV shows.

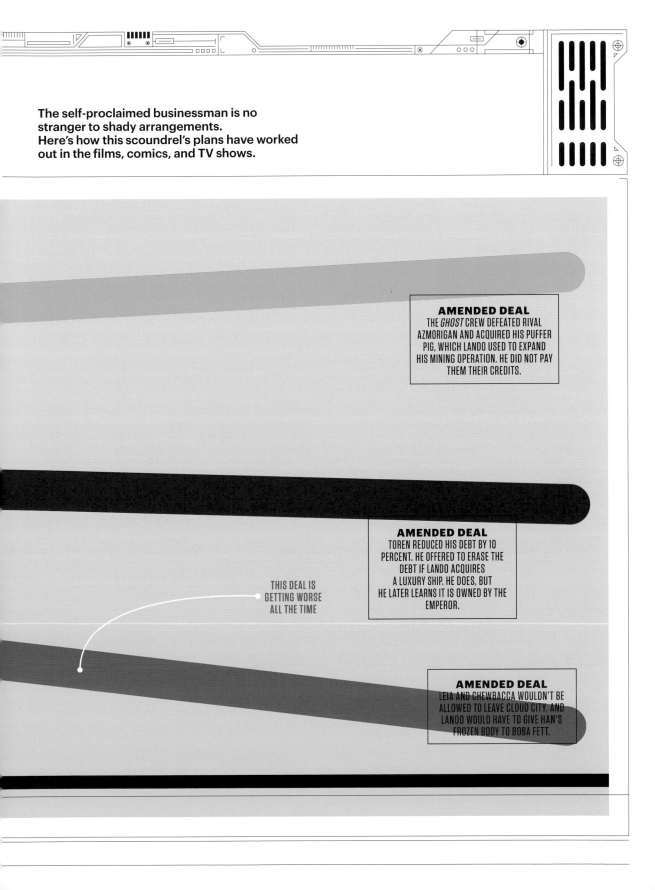

AMENDED DEAL
THE *GHOST* CREW DEFEATED RIVAL AZMORIGAN AND ACQUIRED HIS PUFFER PIG, WHICH LANDO USED TO EXPAND HIS MINING OPERATION. HE DID NOT PAY THEM THEIR CREDITS.

AMENDED DEAL
TOREN REDUCED HIS DEBT BY 10 PERCENT. HE OFFERED TO ERASE THE DEBT IF LANDO ACQUIRES A LUXURY SHIP. HE DOES, BUT HE LATER LEARNS IT IS OWNED BY THE EMPEROR.

THIS DEAL IS GETTING WORSE ALL THE TIME

AMENDED DEAL
LEIA AND CHEWBACCA WOULDN'T BE ALLOWED TO LEAVE CLOUD CITY, AND LANDO WOULD HAVE TO GIVE HAN'S FROZEN BODY TO BOBA FETT.

WHAT LIES BENEATH

1:04.61   0:36.80   0:31.11   5:30.67

0:39.04   01:20:38

First impressions are important. Here's how long (in hours: minutes: seconds) it took different characters to reveal themselves.

● OBI-WAN AND QUI-GON ● QUEEN AMIDALA ● OBI-WAN ● BOUSHH ● DARTH VADER ● FINN ● REY ● KYLO REN

5:52:44

7:47:27

PRECIOUS CARGO

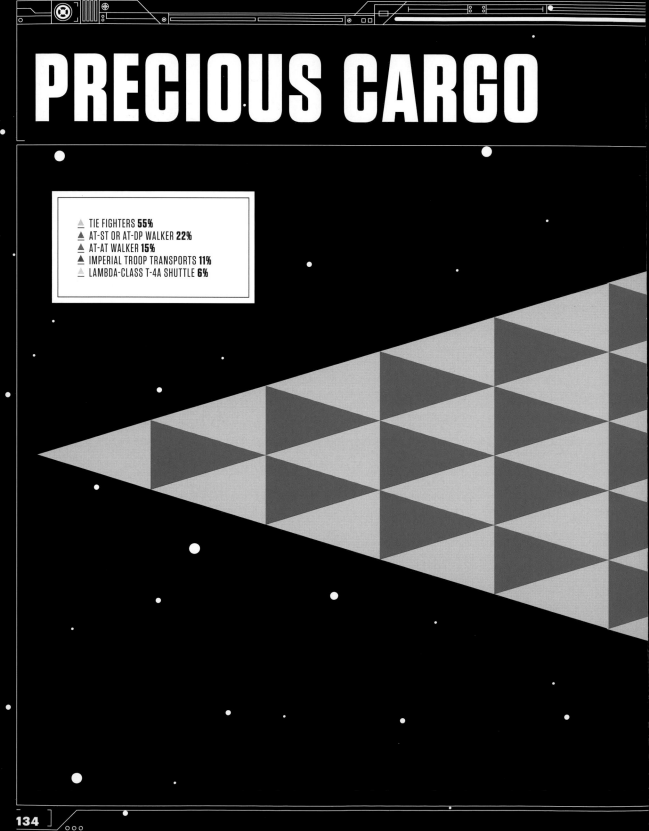

- ▲ TIE FIGHTERS **55%**
- ▲ AT-ST OR AT-DP WALKER **22%**
- ▲ AT-AT WALKER **15%**
- ▲ IMPERIAL TROOP TRANSPORTS **11%**
- ▲ LAMBDA-CLASS T-4A SHUTTLE **6%**

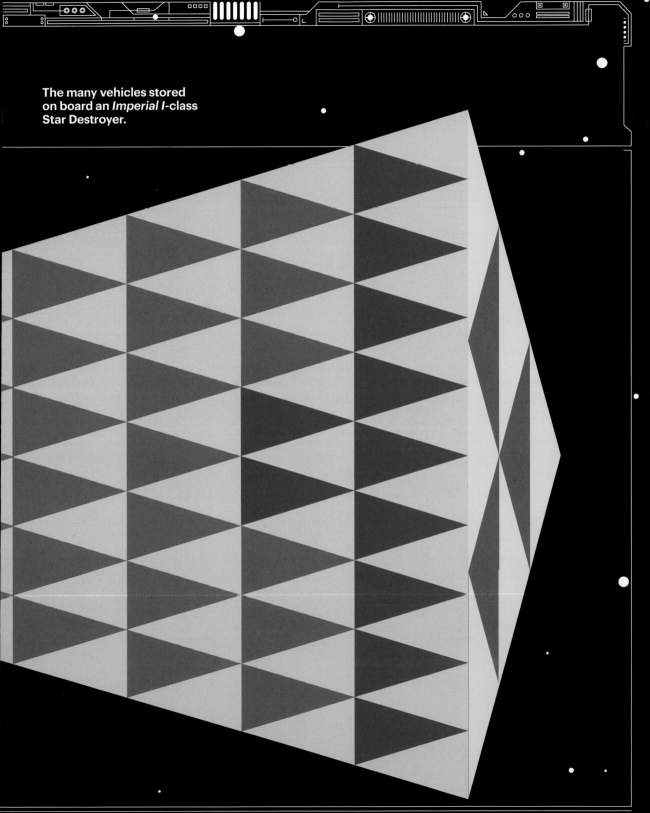

The many vehicles stored
on board an *Imperial I*-class
Star Destroyer.

ALWAYS TWO THERE ARE

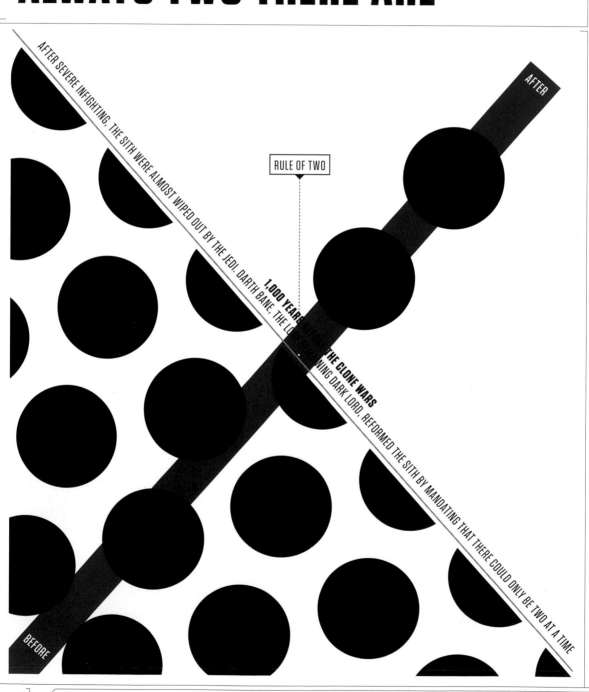

RULE OF TWO

AFTER

AFTER SEVERE INFIGHTING, THE SITH WERE ALMOST WIPED OUT BY THE JEDI. DARTH BANE, THE LO...

1,000 YEARS ... THE CLONE WARS ...NING DARK LORD, REFORMED THE SITH BY MANDATING THAT THERE COULD ONLY BE TWO AT A TIME

BEFORE

WHAT PULLS AT KYLO REN

☐ THE DARK SIDE
◼ THE LIGHT

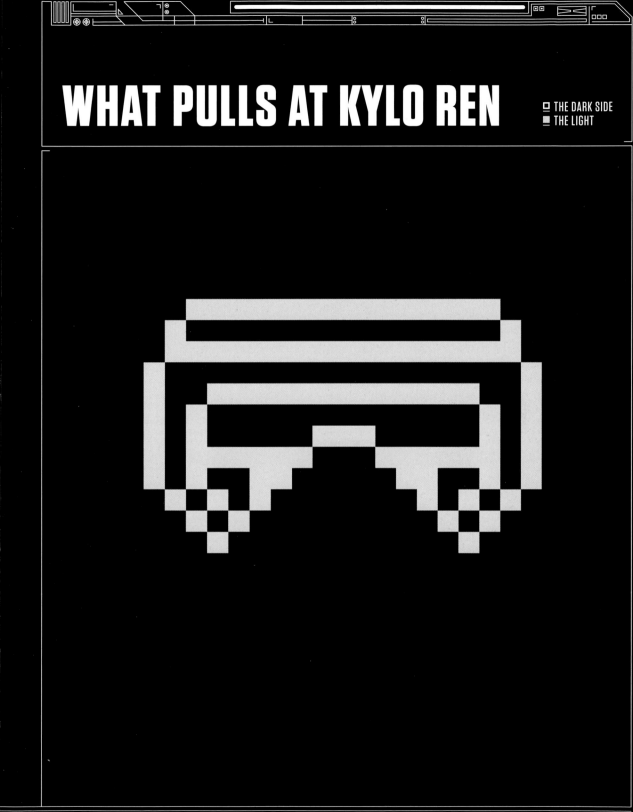

STORMTROOPER UTILITY BELT

What's inside each stormtrooper's hip pack. Now move along.

| WRIST BINDERS (LIKE HANDCUFFS) | BLASTER POWER PACKS FOR E-11 RIFLE | BLASTER POWER PACKS FOR E-11 RIFLE |

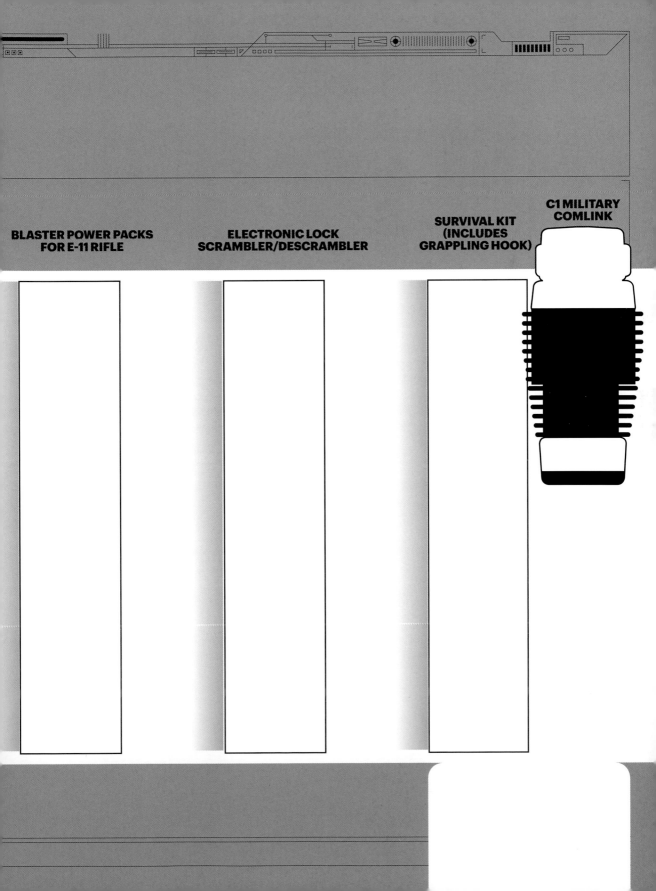

**BLASTER POWER PACKS
FOR E-11 RIFLE**

**ELECTRONIC LOCK
SCRAMBLER/DESCRAMBLER**

**SURVIVAL KIT
(INCLUDES
GRAPPLING HOOK)**

**C1 MILITARY
COMLINK**

GRAND MOFF TARKIN'S MANAGEMENT DECISIONS, ACCORDING TO PRINCESS LEIA

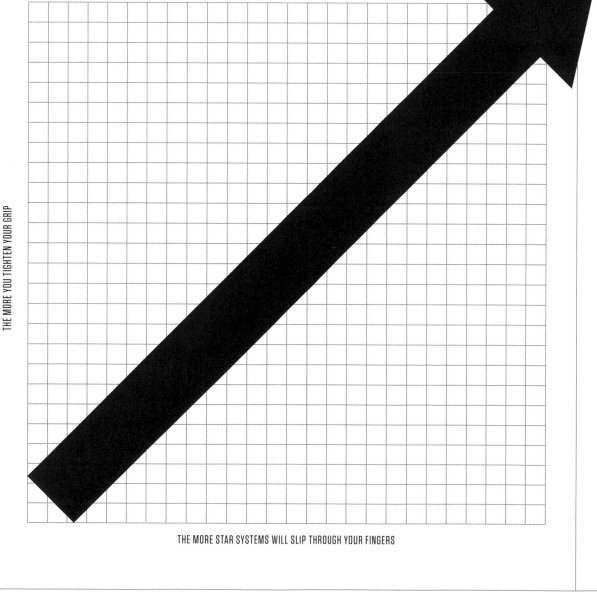

THE MORE YOU TIGHTEN YOUR GRIP

THE MORE STAR SYSTEMS WILL SLIP THROUGH YOUR FINGERS

WALK THIS WAY

Examining the subtle directional cues that foreshadow disaster.

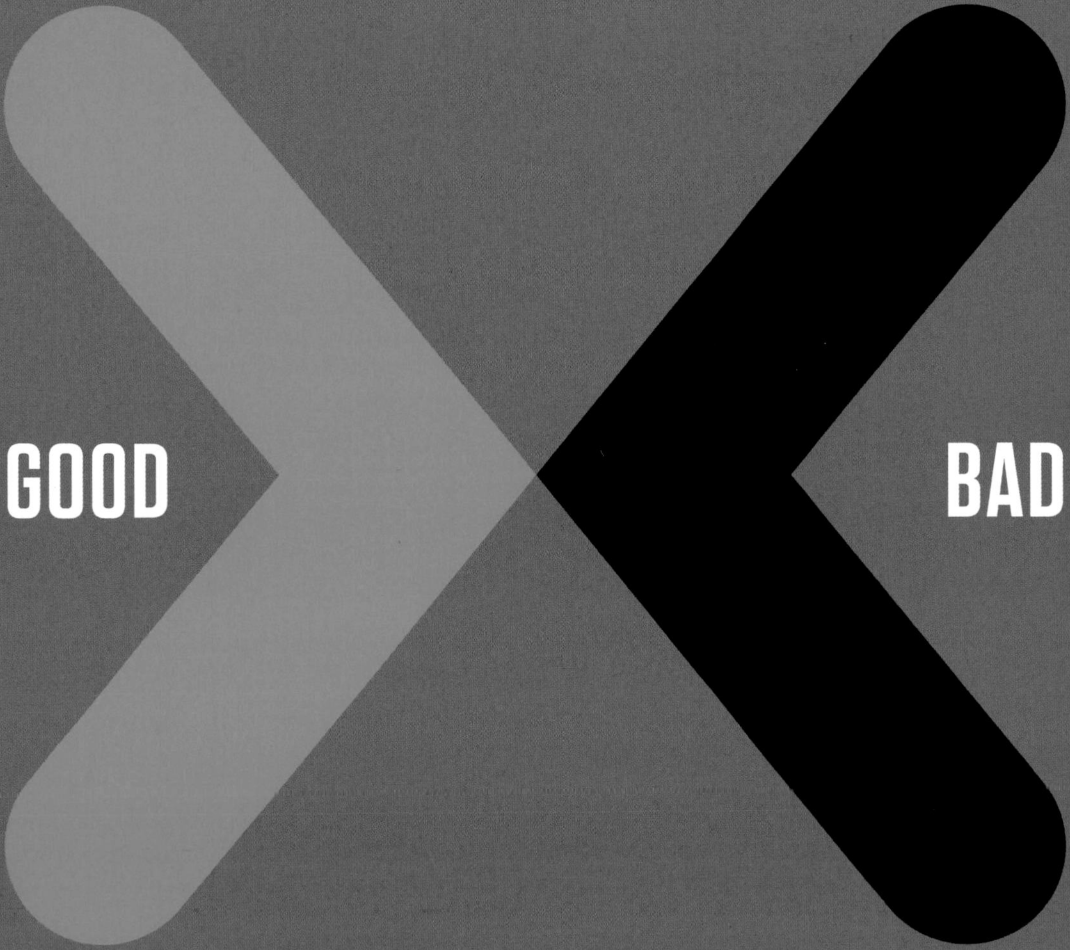

GOOD

BAD

In film, good guys are historically shown moving from left to right on screen. Not only is that how we read, our brains process that movement as natural.

In *The Clone Wars* and *Attack of the Clones*, the clone troopers are mostly shown in battle scenes moving from right to left. This was setup to foreshadow a turn in allegiance—they go on to execute the Jedi.

WHAT A JEDI WANTS

"ADVENTURE. EXCITEMENT. A JEDI CRAVES NOT THESE THINGS." —YODA

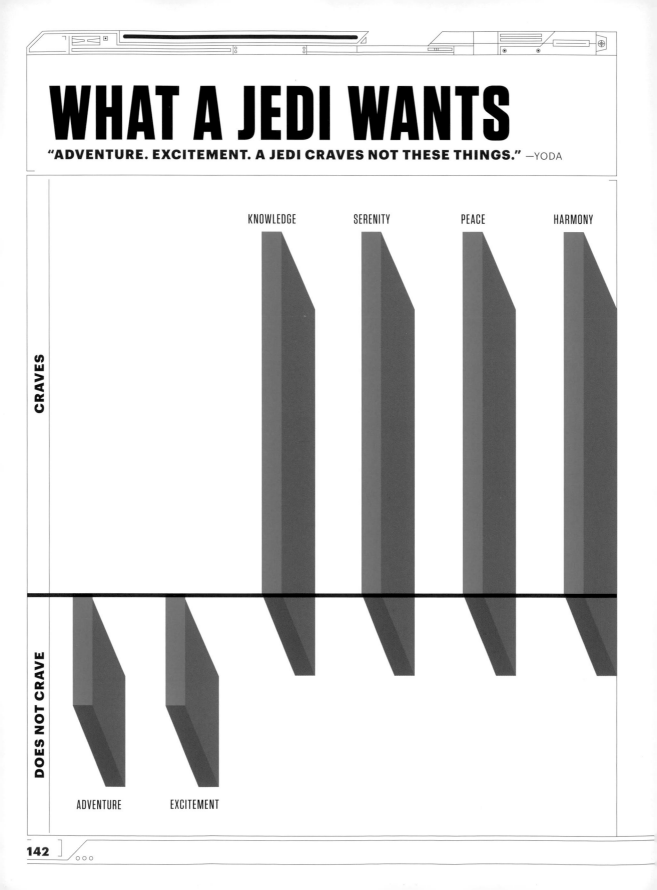

CRAVES

DOES NOT CRAVE

KNOWLEDGE SERENITY PEACE HARMONY

ADVENTURE EXCITEMENT

TAKES THE CAPE

Ranking the most classic coverings.

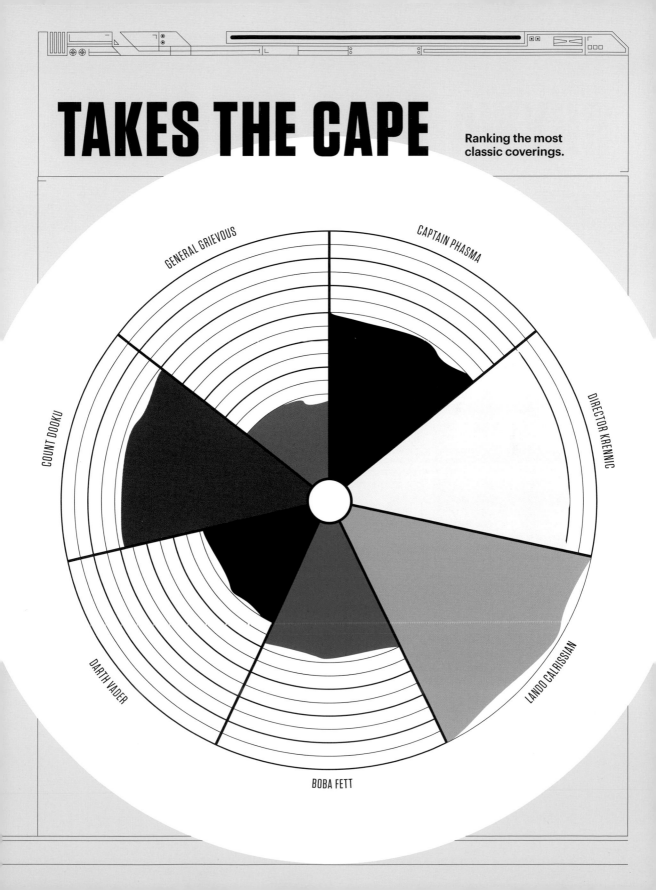

GENERAL GRIEVOUS

CAPTAIN PHASMA

COUNT DOOKU

DIRECTOR KRENNIC

DARTH VADER

LANDO CALRISSIAN

BOBA FETT

SKYWALKER FAMILY TREE

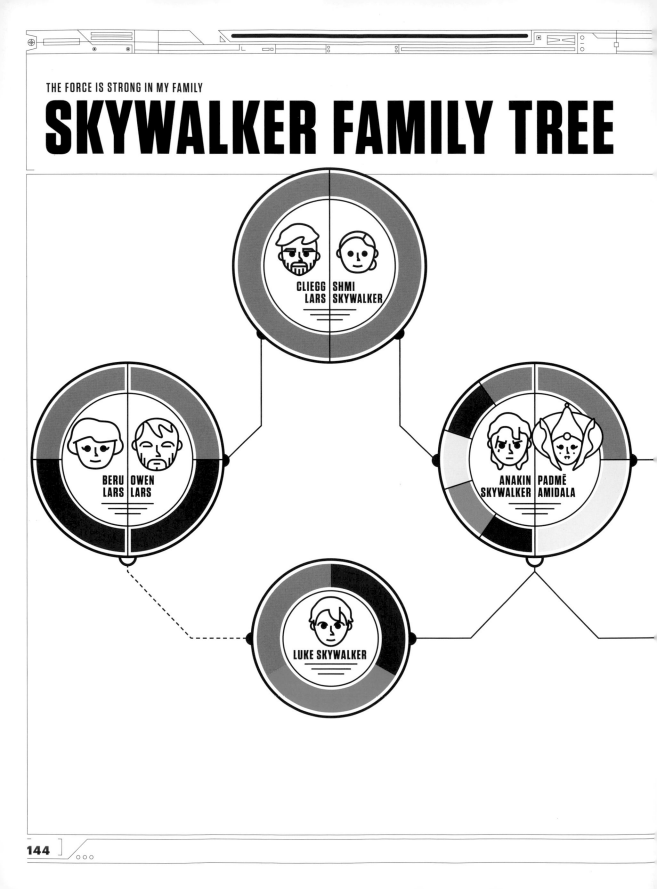

CLIEGG LARS | SHMI SKYWALKER

BERU LARS | OWEN LARS

ANAKIN SKYWALKER | PADMÉ AMIDALA

LUKE SKYWALKER

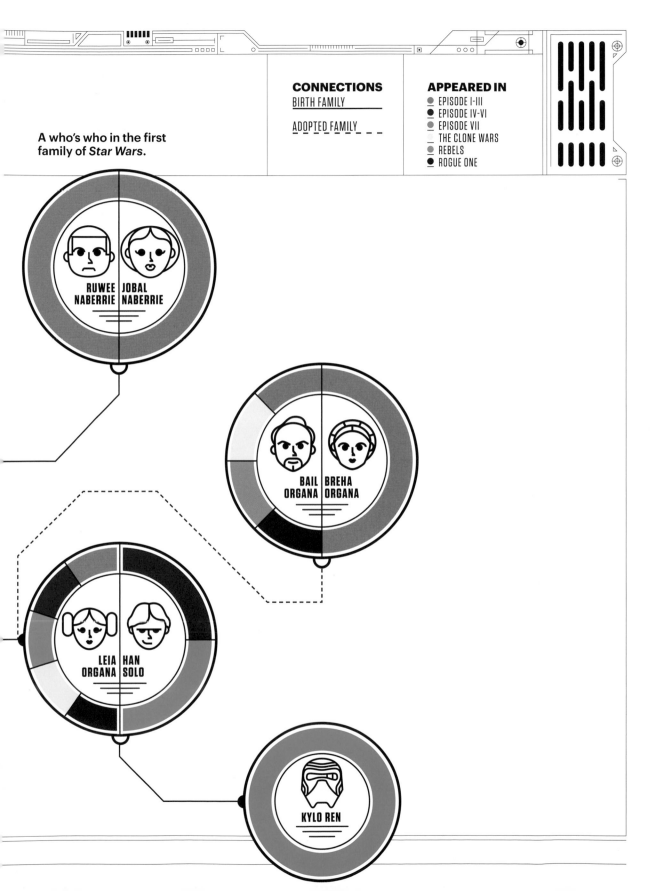

A who's who in the first family of *Star Wars*.

CONNECTIONS

BIRTH FAMILY

ADOPTED FAMILY

APPEARED IN
- EPISODE I–III
- EPISODE IV–VI
- EPISODE VII
- THE CLONE WARS
- REBELS
- ROGUE ONE

RUWEE NABERRIE | JOBAL NABERRIE

BAIL ORGANA | BREHA ORGANA

LEIA ORGANA | HAN SOLO

KYLO REN

THE BOONTA EVE CLASSIC

The final results from the podrace that finally earned Anakin first place—and his freedom.

	STARTING LINE	MIDDLE OF LAP 1	LAP 1
ALDAR BEEDO			
RATTS TYERELL			
SEBULBA			
MAWHONIC			
DUD BOLT			
ANAKIN SKYWALKER			
CLEGG HOLDFAST			
EBE E. ENDOCOTT			
GASGANO			
BOLES ROOR			
TEEMTO PAGALIES			
ELAN MAK			
MARS GUO			
ARK "BUMPY" ROOSE			
NEVA KEE			
WAN SANDAGE			
ODY MANDRELL			
BEN QUADINAROS	POWER COUPLING MALFUNCTION AT START	ENGINE EXPLOSION DURING PIT STOP	

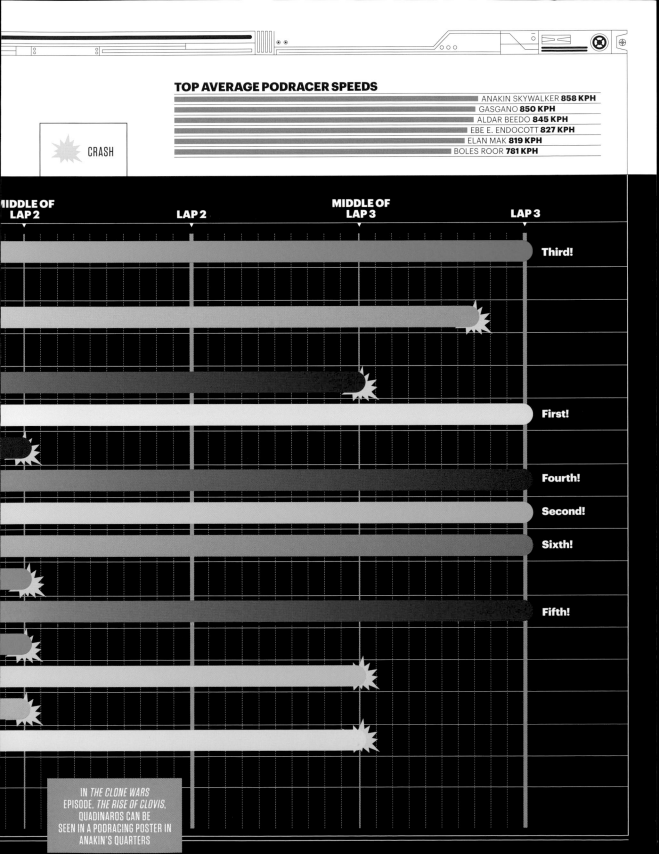

TOP AVERAGE PODRACER SPEEDS

ANAKIN SKYWALKER	**858 KPH**
GASGANO	**850 KPH**
ALDAR BEEDO	**845 KPH**
EBE E. ENDOCOTT	**827 KPH**
ELAN MAK	**819 KPH**
BOLES ROOR	**781 KPH**

CRASH

MIDDLE OF LAP 2

LAP 2

MIDDLE OF LAP 3

LAP 3

Third!

First!

Fourth!

Second!

Sixth!

Fifth!

IN *THE CLONE WARS* EPISODE, *THE RISE OF CLOVIS*, QUADINAROS CAN BE SEEN IN A PODRACING POSTER IN ANAKIN'S QUARTERS

MAZ KANATA

- ATTRACTION TO RELICS ASSOCIATED WITH THE FORCE
- ATTRACTION TO PIRATES
- ATTRACTION TO CHEWBACCA

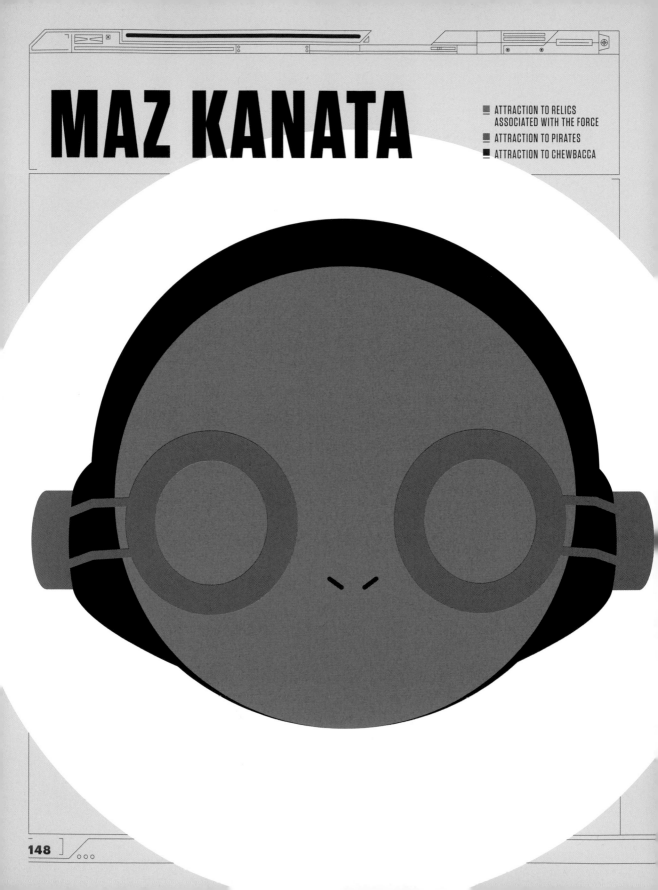

TRADE-IN VALUE

What Unkar Plutt offers Rey for her scavaging efforts.

○ OFFER FOR SALVAGE ON DAY 1   ◑ OFFER FOR SALVAGE ON DAY 2   ● OFFER FOR BB-8

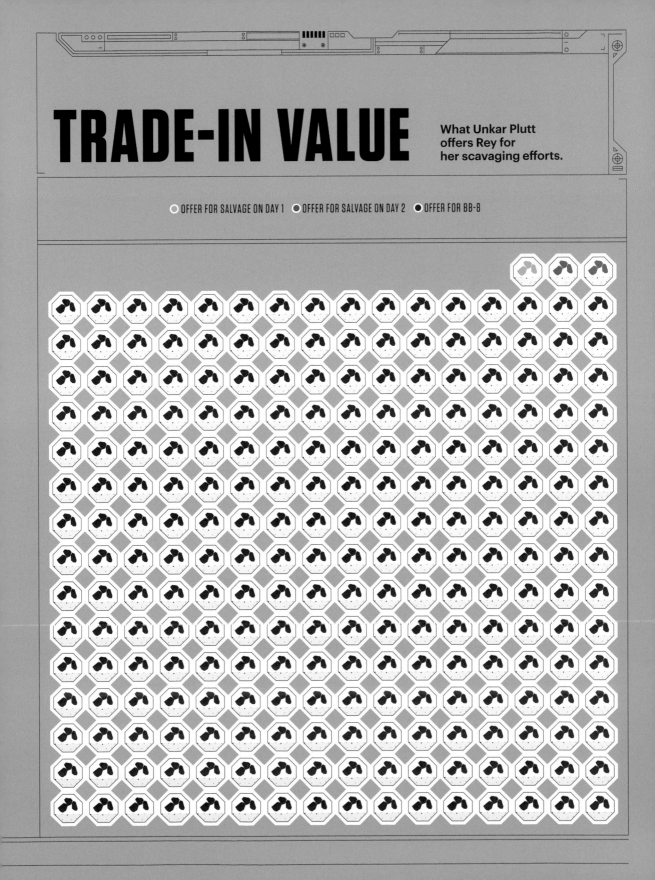

CREDITS RULE EVERYTHING AROUND ME

- **35,000** AMOUNT JABBA AGREES TO PAY FOR THE MIGHTY CHEWBACCA
- **20,000** AMOUNT QUI-GON JINN OFFERS FOR A T-14 HYPERDRIVE GENERATOR
- **17,000** AMOUNT OBI-WAN OFFERS TO HAN TO FLY HE AND LUKE TO ALDERAAN
- **2,000** AMOUNT LUKE RECEIVES WHEN HE SELLS HIS SPEEDER
- **50,000** HAN BORROWS FROM KANJIKLUB
- **50,000** HAN BORROWS FROM THE GUAVIAN DEATH GANG

Credits (or "creds") were a standardized form of currency in the Galactic Republic and Galactic Empire. Having a stanardized currency was important, so that the thousands of planets in the Empire could trade. Credits could be stored on credit chips or used like cash with credit ignots, which looked like small gold or silver bars.

CURRENCY CONVERTER

The Wupiupi was the primary form of currency used by the Hutts on Tatooine and came in the form of gold coins. The Wupiupi had several denominations:

ONE CREDIT IS WORTH:

WUPIUPI
ONE WUPIUPI IS WORTH ROUGHLY .625 CREDITS

TRUGUT
ONE TRUGUT IS WORTH 10 WUPIUPI

PEGGAT
ONE PEGGAT IS WORTH 40 CREDITS

5,000
PAYMENT LUKE AND HAN RECEIVE FOR HAULING NERFS

224,190
HAN OWES JABBA

60,000
VALUE OF THE BOUNTY ON LUKE'S HEAD

50,000
VALUE OF THE BOUNTY ON HAN'S HEAD

VISION QUEST

MAZ KANATA'S CASTLE	CLOUD CITY	OUTSIDE TEMPLE

SCENE

The storage room of Maz Kanata's castle begins to darken.

Rey is in a hallway deep inside Cloud City, which is where Luke fought Darth Vader in Episode V.

Luke and R2-D2 are outside a temple. There is a fire nearby.

AUDIO

DARTH VADER BREATHING

LIGHTSABER TURNS ON

YODA: "IT'S ENERGY..."

YOUNG REY: "NOOOO!"

YODA: "...SURROUNDS US, AND BINDS US"

LUKE: "NOOOO!"

OBI-WAN: "YOU WILL BE TEMPTED"

OBI-WAN: "BUT YOU CANNOT CONTROL IT"

YODA: "...SURROUNDS US"

THE PHANTOM MENACE	*ATTACK OF THE CLONES*	*REVENGE OF THE SITH*	

When Rey finds Luke's missing lightsaber in *The Force Awakens*, she's hit with a vision. (The lightsaber was once Anakin's and then Luke's. Luke lost it during his fight with Darth Vader.) Below is a breakdown of all the hidden references stuffed into Rey's 51-second, lightsaber-induced montage.

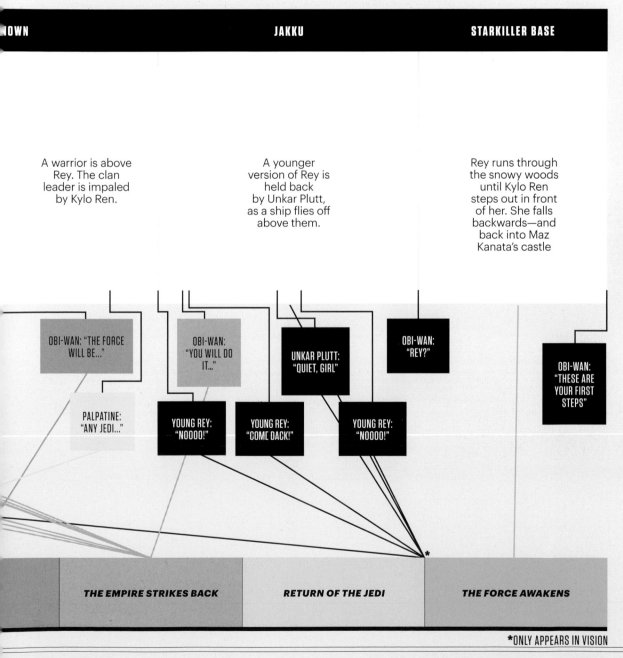

...NOWN

JAKKU

STARKILLER BASE

A warrior is above Rey. The clan leader is impaled by Kylo Ren.

A younger version of Rey is held back by Unkar Plutt, as a ship flies off above them.

Rey runs through the snowy woods until Kylo Ren steps out in front of her. She falls backwards—and back into Maz Kanata's castle

OBI-WAN: "THE FORCE WILL BE..."

OBI-WAN: "YOU WILL DO IT..."

UNKAR PLUTT: "QUIET, GIRL"

OBI-WAN: "REY?"

OBI-WAN: "THESE ARE YOUR FIRST STEPS"

PALPATINE: "ANY JEDI..."

YOUNG REY: "NOOOO!"

YOUNG REY: "COME DACK!"

YOUNG REY: "NOOOO!"

THE EMPIRE STRIKES BACK

RETURN OF THE JEDI

THE FORCE AWAKENS

*ONLY APPEARS IN VISION

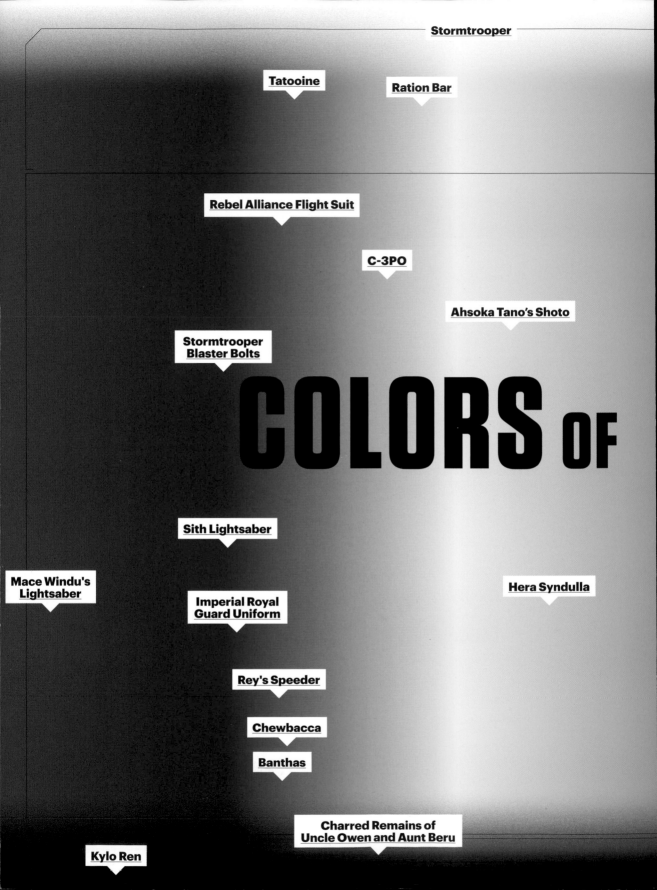

Stormtrooper

Tatooine

Ration Bar

Rebel Alliance Flight Suit

C-3PO

Ahsoka Tano's Shoto

Stormtrooper Blaster Bolts

COLORS OF

Sith Lightsaber

Mace Windu's Lightsaber

Hera Syndulla

Imperial Royal Guard Uniform

Rey's Speeder

Chewbacca

Banthas

Charred Remains of Uncle Owen and Aunt Beru

Kylo Ren

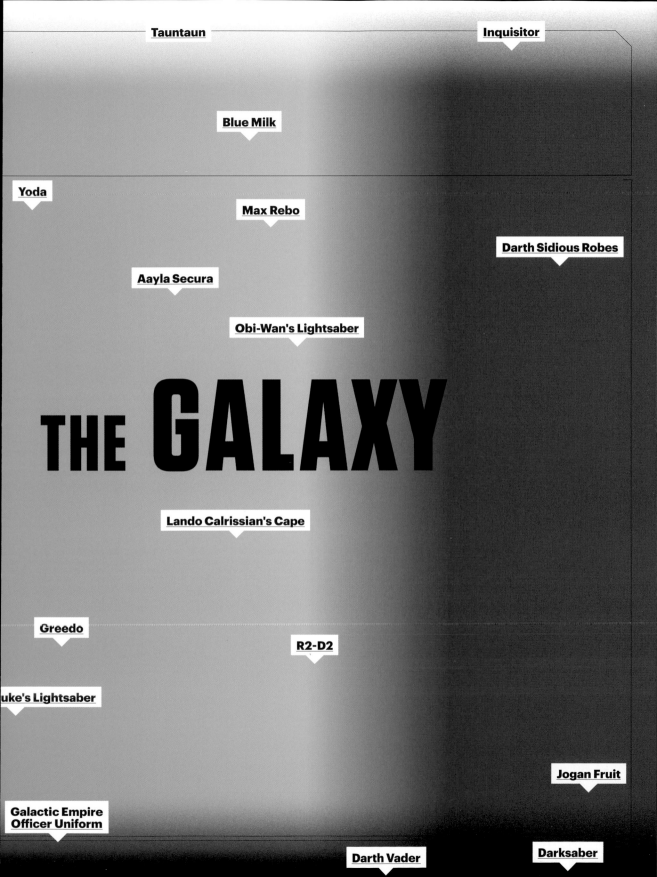

THE **GALAXY**

Tauntaun

Inquisitor

Blue Milk

Yoda

Max Rebo

Darth Sidious Robes

Aayla Secura

Obi-Wan's Lightsaber

Lando Calrissian's Cape

Greedo

R2-D2

uke's Lightsaber

Jogan Fruit

Galactic Empire
Officer Uniform

Darth Vader

Darksaber

MASTER CLASS

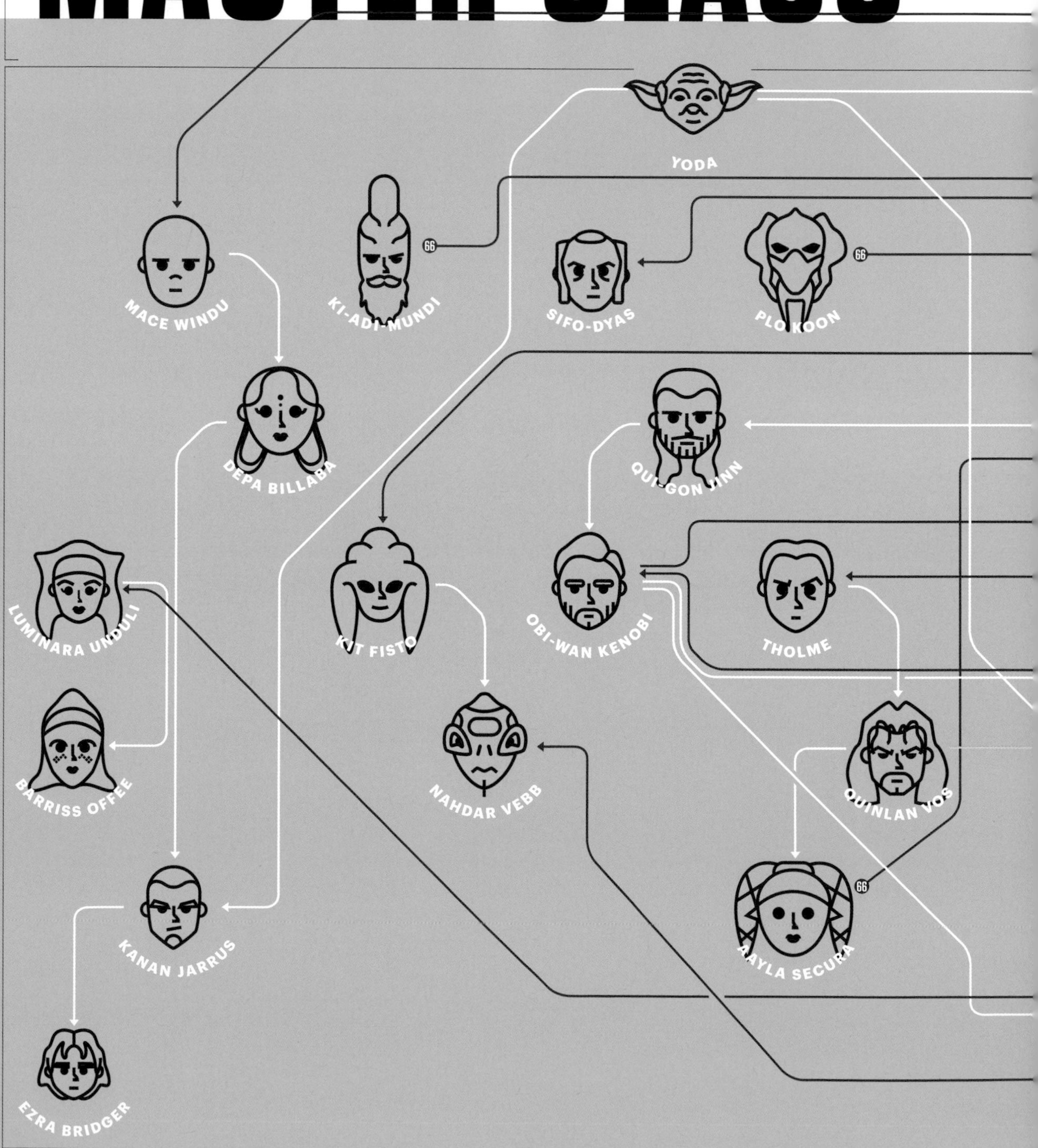

YODA

MACE WINDU

KI-ADI-MUNDI

SIFO-DYAS

PLO KOON

DEPA BILLABA

QUI-GON JINN

LUMINARA UNDULI

KIT FISTO

OBI-WAN KENOBI

THOLME

BARRISS OFFEE

NAHDAR VEBB

QUINLAN VOS

KANAN JARRUS

AAYLA SECURA

EZRA BRIDGER

Every master and apprentice relationship.

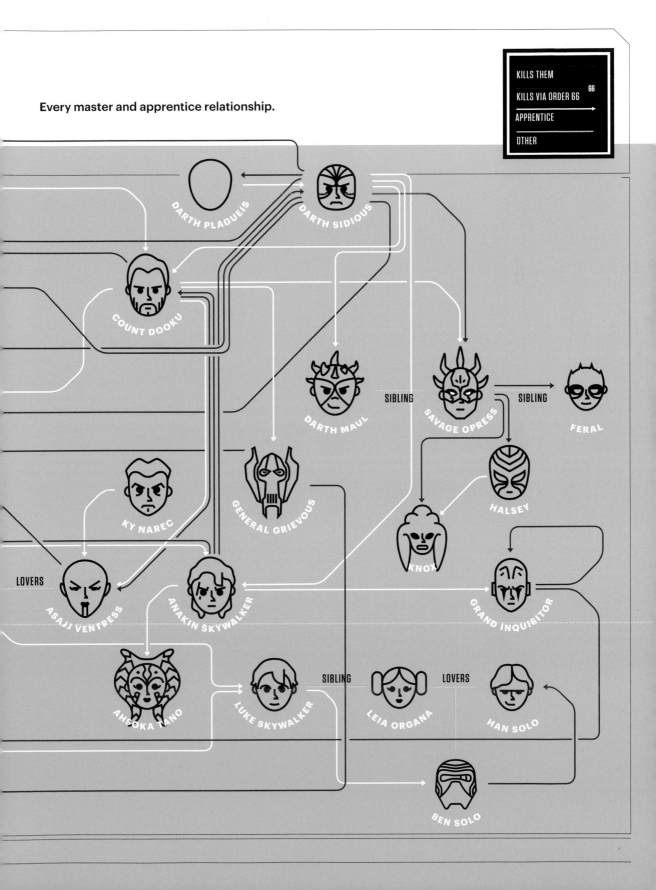

KILLS THEM
KILLS VIA ORDER 66 [66] →
APPRENTICE
OTHER

DARTH PLAGUEIS
DARTH SIDIOUS
COUNT DOOKU
DARTH MAUL
SIBLING
SAVAGE OPRESS
SIBLING
FERAL
HALSEY
KY NAREC
GENERAL GRIEVOUS
KNOX
GRAND INQUISITOR
LOVERS
ASAJJ VENTRESS
ANAKIN SKYWALKER
AHSOKA TANO
LUKE SKYWALKER
SIBLING
LEIA ORGANA
LOVERS
HAN SOLO
BEN SOLO

GREEDO'S LUCK

■ HE'S LUCKY HE FOUND HAN FIRST

■ HE'S UNLUCKY THAT HE MISSES WHEN HE SHOOTS HAN

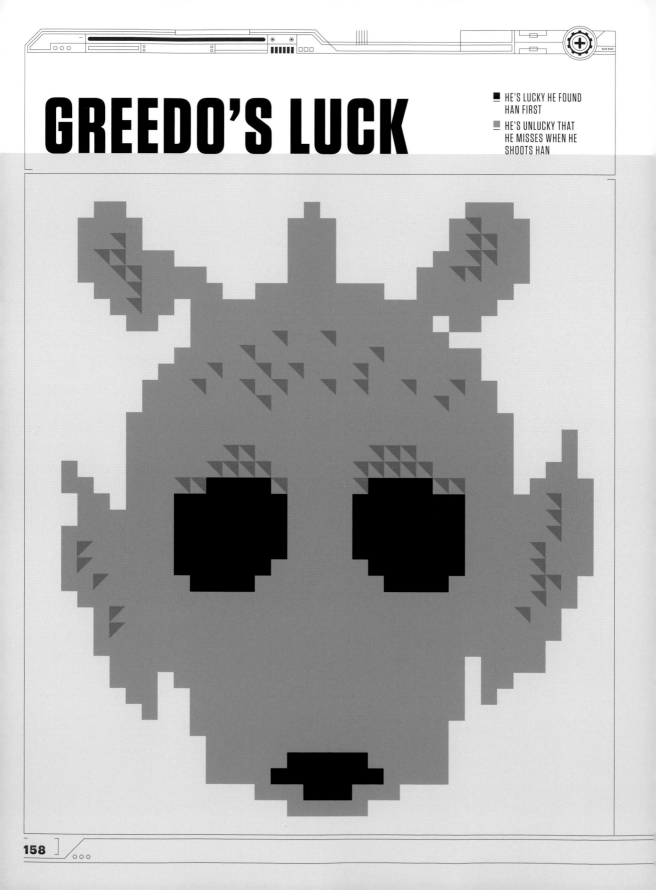

ADMIRAL ACKBAR'S OUTTAKES

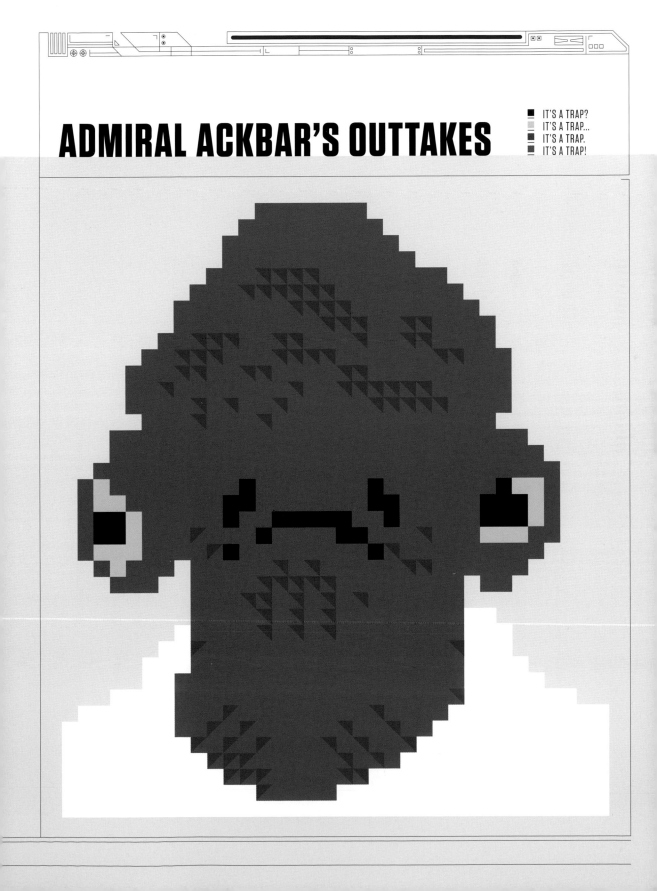

IT'S A TRAP?
IT'S A TRAP...
IT'S A TRAP.
IT'S A TRAP!

AREN'T YOU A LITTLE SHORT

From Ewoks to Wookiees, these characters stand tall.

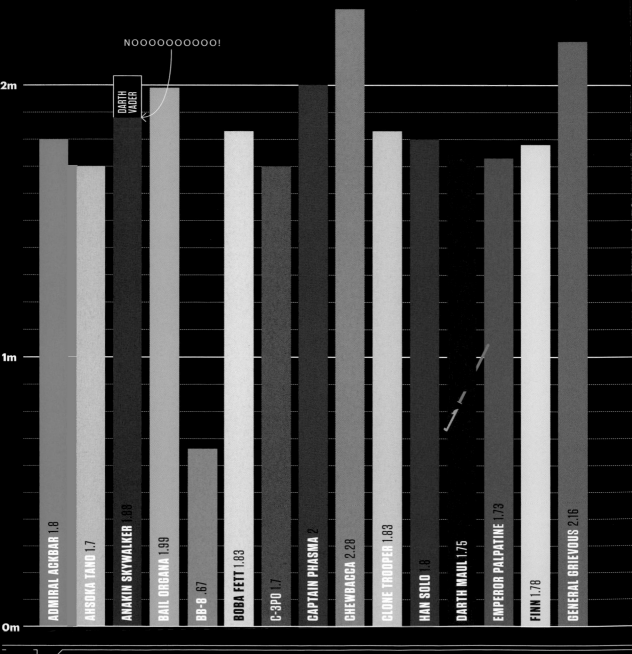

NOOOOOOOOOO!

DARTH VADER

2m

1m

0m

ADMIRAL ACKBAR 1.8

AHSOKA TANO 1.7

ANAKIN SKYWALKER 1.88

BAIL ORGANA 1.99

BB-8 .67

BOBA FETT 1.83

C-3PO 1.7

CAPTAIN PHASMA 2

CHEWBACCA 2.28

CLONE TROOPER 1.83

HAN SOLO 1.8

DARTH MAUL 1.75

EMPEROR PALPATINE 1.73

FINN 1.78

GENERAL GRIEVOUS 2.16

FOR A STORMTROOPER?

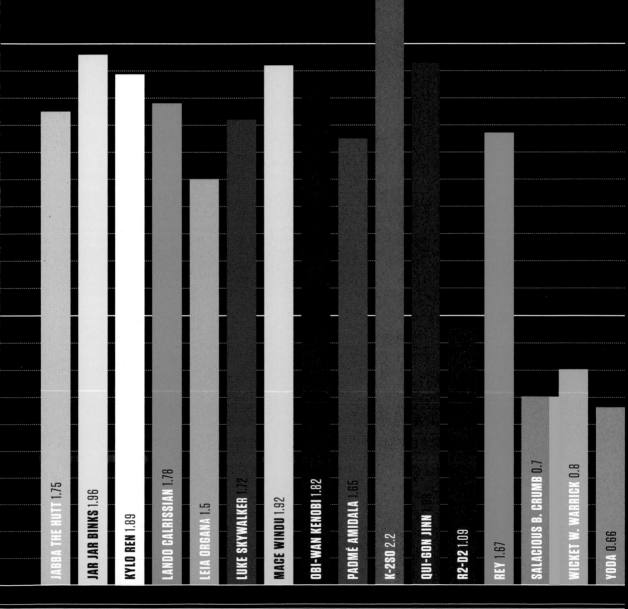

JABBA THE HUTT 1.75
JAR JAR BINKS 1.96
KYLO REN 1.89
LANDO CALRISSIAN 1.78
LEIA ORGANA 1.5
LUKE SKYWALKER 1.72
MACE WINDU 1.92
OBI-WAN KENOBI 1.82
PADMÉ AMIDALA 1.65
K-2SO 2.2
QUI-GON JINN
R2-D2 1.09
REY 1.67
SALACIOUS B. CRUMB 0.7
WICKET W. WARRICK 0.8
YODA 0.66

NAMES THAT ARE OUT OF THIS WORLD

Special effects and design weren't the only creative approaches to characters. The names are just as inventive.

COUNT DOOKU
ATTACK OF THE CLONES, REVENGE OF THE SITH
A Jedi Master who became the apprentice to Darth Sidious.

WICKET W. WARRICK
RETURN OF THE JEDI
An Ewok scout who befriends Leia.

BIB FORTUNA
RETURN OF THE JEDI
A Twi'lek who served as majordomo (representative) to Jabba the Hutt.

PONDA BABA
A NEW HOPE
Patron of the Mos Eisley cantina who had the misfortune of drawing on Obi-Wan.

ELAN SLEAZEBAGGANO
ATTACK OF THE CLONES
Obi-Wan uses the mind trick to force this death stick dealer to go home and rethink his life.

IN ORBIT

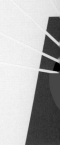

BIGGS DARKLIGHTER
A NEW HOPE
Luke's childhood friend and member of Red Squadron.

JAR JAR BINKS
THE PHANTOM MENACE,
ATTACK OF THE CLONES,
REVENGE OF THE SITH
Heesa a naive Gungan from Naboo who becomes a Senator.

DROOPY MCCOOL
A NEW HOPE
The lead horn player of the Max Rebo band, located at Jabba the Hutt's palace.

JEK PORKINS
A NEW HOPE
Red Squadron starfighter who dies during the Battle of Yavin.

SALACIOUS B. CRUMB
RETURN OF THE JEDI
This court jester for Jabba the Hutt has a distinctive laugh.

LIGHTYEARS AWAY

VEHICLE aCRONYMs

aCRONYMs

Your guide to four-letter naming conventions. Sorry, AT-ACT (All Terrain Armored Cargo Transport)!

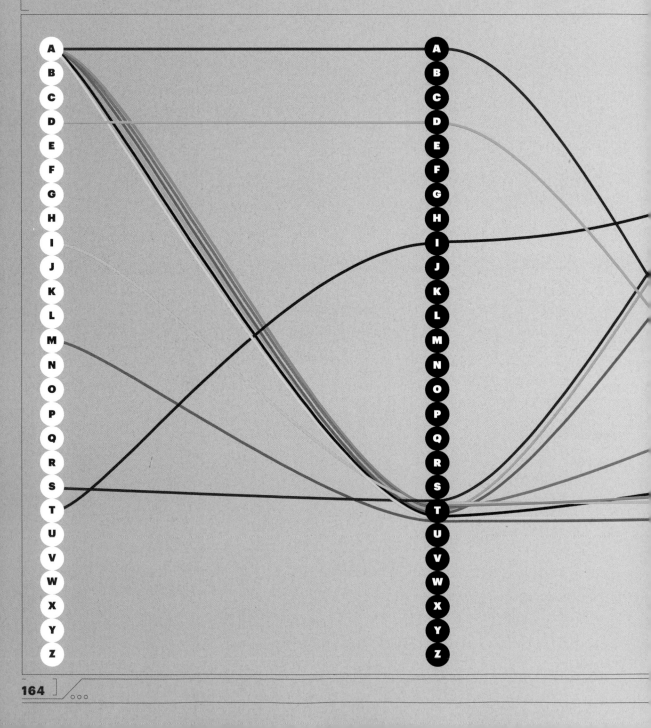

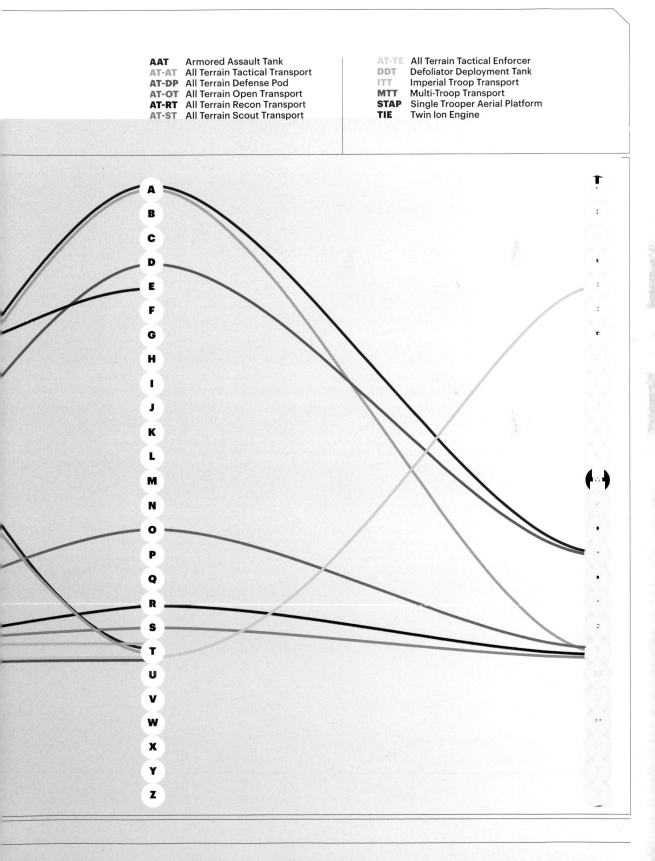

AAT	Armored Assault Tank
AT-AT	All Terrain Tactical Transport
AT-DP	All Terrain Defense Pod
AT-OT	All Terrain Open Transport
AT-RT	All Terrain Recon Transport
AT-ST	All Terrain Scout Transport

AT-TE	All Terrain Tactical Enforcer
DDT	Defoliator Deployment Tank
ITT	Imperial Troop Transport
MTT	Multi-Troop Transport
STAP	Single Trooper Aerial Platform
TIE	Twin Ion Engine

WHAT'S IN A NAME

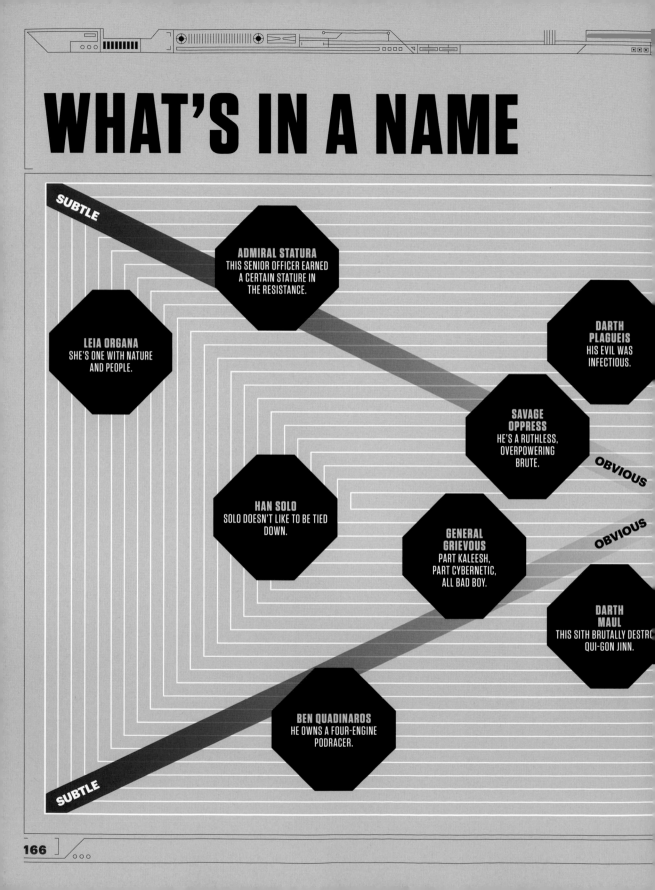

SUBTLE

ADMIRAL STATURA
THIS SENIOR OFFICER EARNED A CERTAIN STATURE IN THE RESISTANCE.

LEIA ORGANA
SHE'S ONE WITH NATURE AND PEOPLE.

DARTH PLAGUEIS
HIS EVIL WAS INFECTIOUS.

SAVAGE OPPRESS
HE'S A RUTHLESS, OVERPOWERING BRUTE.

OBVIOUS

HAN SOLO
SOLO DOESN'T LIKE TO BE TIED DOWN.

GENERAL GRIEVOUS
PART KALEESH, PART CYBERNETIC, ALL BAD BOY.

OBVIOUS

DARTH MAUL
THIS SITH BRUTALLY DESTRO
QUI-GON JINN.

BEN QUADINAROS
HE OWNS A FOUR-ENGINE PODRACER.

SUBTLE

A name can say a lot about a person. Here are some names that telegraph the character's personality.

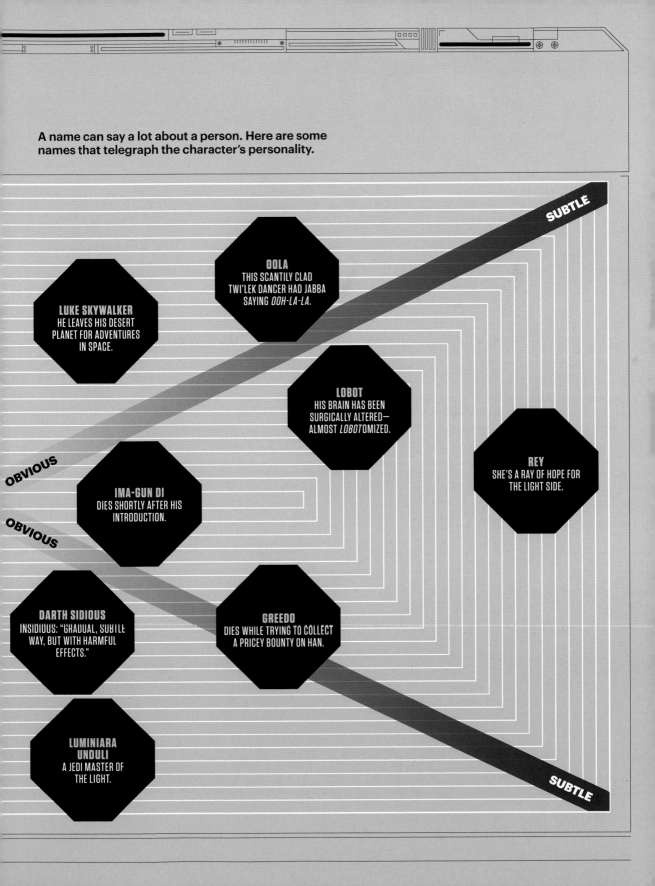

SUBTLE

OBVIOUS

OBVIOUS

SUBTLE

OOLA
THIS SCANTILY CLAD TWI'LEK DANCER HAD JABBA SAYING *OOH-LA-LA.*

LUKE SKYWALKER
HE LEAVES HIS DESERT PLANET FOR ADVENTURES IN SPACE.

LOBOT
HIS BRAIN HAS BEEN SURGICALLY ALTERED—ALMOST *LOBOT*OMIZED.

REY
SHE'S A RAY OF HOPE FOR THE LIGHT SIDE.

IMA-GUN DI
DIES SHORTLY AFTER HIS INTRODUCTION.

DARTH SIDIOUS
INSIDIOUS: "GRADUAL, SUBTLE WAY, BUT WITH HARMFUL EFFECTS."

GREEDO
DIES WHILE TRYING TO COLLECT A PRICEY BOUNTY ON HAN.

LUMINIARA UNDULI
A JEDI MASTER OF THE LIGHT.

THE CLONE WARS EPISODES, IN ORDER

ORIGINAL AIRDATE ORDER

CHRONOLOGICAL ORDER

#	Episode	SEASON 1	SEASON 2	SEASON 3	SEASON 4	SEASON 5	SEASON 6
1	Cat and Mouse			♦ EP. 16			
2	Hidden Enemy		♦ EP. 16				
3	*The Clone Wars* theatrical film	♦ THEATRICAL FILM					
4	Clone Cadets			♦ EP. 1			
5	Supply Lines			♦ EP. 3			
6	Ambush	♦ EP. 1					
7	Rising Malevolence	♦ EP. 2					
8	Shadow of Malevolence	♦ EP. 3					
9	Destroy Malevolence	♦ EP. 4					
10	Rookies	♦ EP. 5					
11	Downfall of a Droid	♦ EP. 6					
12	Duel of the Droids	♦ EP. 7					
13	Bombad Jedi	♦ EP. 8					
14	Cloak of Darkness	♦ EP. 9					
15	Lair of Grievous	♦ EP. 10					
16	Dooku Captured	♦ EP. 11					
17	The Gungan General	♦ EP. 12					
18	Jedi Crash	♦ EP. 13					
19	Defenders of Peace	♦ EP. 14					
20	Trespass	♦ EP. 15					
21	Blue Shadow Virus	♦ EP. 17					
22	Mystery of a Thousand Moons	♦ EP. 18					
23	Storm over Ryloth	♦ EP. 19					
24	Innocents of Ryloth	♦ EP. 20					
25	Liberty on Ryloth	♦ EP. 21					
26	Holocron Heist		♦ EP. 1				
27	Cargo of Doom		♦ EP. 2				
28	Children of the Force		♦ EP. 3				
29	Bounty Hunters		♦ EP. 17				
30	The Zillo Beast		♦ EP. 18				
31	The Zillo Beast Strikes Back		♦ EP. 19				
32	Senate Spy		♦ EP. 4				
33	Landing at Point Rain		♦ EP. 5				
34	Weapons Factory		♦ EP. 6				
35	Legacy of Terror		♦ EP. 7				
36	Brain Invaders		♦ EP. 8				
37	Grievous Intrigue		♦ EP. 9				
38	The Deserter		♦ EP. 10				
39	Lightsaber Lost		♦ EP. 11				
40	The Mandalore Plot		♦ EP. 12				
41	Voyage of Temptation		♦ EP. 13				
42	Duchess of Mandalore		♦ EP. 14				
43	Death Trap		♦ EP. 20				
44	R2 Come Home		♦ EP. 21				
45	Lethal Trackdown		♦ EP. 22				
46	Corruption			♦ EP. 5			
47	The Academy			♦ EP. 6			
48	Assassin			♦ EP. 7			
49	ARC Troopers			♦ EP. 2			
50	Sphere of Influence			♦ EP. 4			
51	Evil Plans			♦ EP. 8			
52	Hostage Crisis		♦ EP. 22				
53	Hunt for Ziro			♦ EP. 9			
54	Heroes on Both Side			♦ EP. 10			
55	Pursuit of Peace			♦ EP. 11			
56	Senate Murders		♦ EP. 15				
57	Nightsisters			♦ EP. 12			
58	Monster			♦ EP. 13			
59	Witches of the Mist			♦ EP. 14			
60	Overlords			♦ EP. 15			
61	Altar of Mortis			♦ EP. 16			

ORIGINAL AIRDATE ORDER

CHRONOLOGICAL ORDER		Title	SEASON 1	SEASON 2	SEASON 3	SEASON 4	SEASON 5	SEASON 6
	62	Ghosts of Mortis				EP. 17		
	63	The Citadel				EP. 18		
	64	Counterattack				EP. 19		
	65	Citadel Rescue				EP. 20		
	66	Padawan Lost				EP. 21		
	67	Wookiee Hunt				EP. 22		
	68	Water War				EP. 1		
	69	Gungan Attack				EP. 2		
	70	Prisoners				EP. 3		
	71	Shadow Warrior				EP. 4		
	72	Mercy Mission				EP. 5		
	73	Nomad Droids				EP. 6		
	74	Darkness on Umbara				EP. 7		
	75	The General				EP. 8		
	76	Plan of Dissent				EP. 9		
	77	Carnage of Krell				EP. 10		
	78	Kidnapped				EP. 11		
	79	Slaves of the Republic				EP. 12		
	80	Escape from Kadavo				EP. 13		
	81	A Friend In Need				EP. 14		
	82	Deception				EP. 15		
	83	Friends and Enemies				EP. 16		
	84	The Box				EP. 17		
	85	Crisis on Naboo				EP. 18		
	86	Massacre				EP. 19		
	87	Bounty				EP. 20		
	88	Brothers				EP. 21		
	89	Revenge				EP. 22		
	90	A War on Two Fronts					EP. 2	
	91	Front Runners					EP. 3	
	92	The Soft War					EP. 4	
	93	Tipping Points					EP. 5	
	94	The Gathering					EP. 6	
	95	A Test of Strength					EP. 7	
	96	Bound for Rescue					EP. 8	
	97	A Necessary Bond					EP. 9	
	98	Secret Weapons					EP. 10	
	99	A Sunny Day in the Void					EP. 11	
	100	Missing in Action					EP. 12	
	101	Point of No Return					EP. 13	
	102	Revival					EP. 1	
	103	Eminence					EP. 14	
	104	Shades of Reason					EP. 15	
	105	The Lawless					EP. 16	
	106	Sabotage					EP. 17	
	107	The Jedi Who Knew Too Much					EP. 18	
	108	To Catch a Jedi					EP. 19	
	109	The Wrong Jedi					EP. 20	
	110	The Unknown						EP. 1
	111	Conspiracy						EP. 2
	112	Fugitive						EP. 3
	113	Orders						EP. 4
	114	An Old Friend						EP. 5
	115	The Rise of Clovis						EP. 6
	116	Crisis at the Heart						EP. 7
	117	The Disappeared						EP. 8
	118	The Disappeared: Part II						EP. 9
	119	The Lost One						EP. 10
	120	Voices						EP. 11
	121	Destiny						EP. 12
	122	Sacrifice						EP. 13

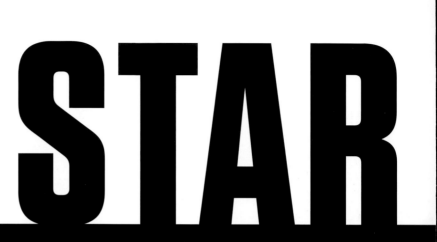

It surrounds us and binds us—yes, the Force, but also grammar. Here's a hidden grammatical pattern between the film titles of the original and prequel trilogies.

STAR

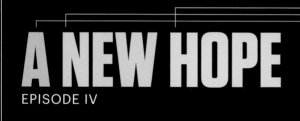

A NEW HOPE
EPISODE IV

THE EMPIRE STRIKES BACK
EPISODE V

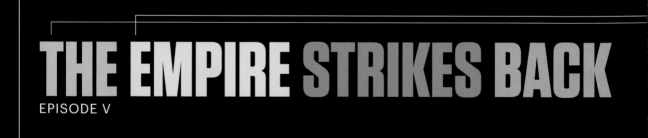

RETURN OF THE JEDI
EPISODE VI

THE ORIGINAL TITLE OF EPISODE VI WAS *REVENGE OF THE JEDI*

WORDS

■ ARTICLE   ■ ADJECTIVE   ■ NOUN   ■ VERB   ■ PREPOSITION   ■ ADVERB

THE PHANTOM MENACE
EPISODE I

ATTACK OF THE CLONES
EPISODE II

REVENGE OF THE SITH
EPISODE III

HISTORY REPEATING

	RAISED IN DESERT	GAVE VALUABLE INTEL TO A DROID	HAD ANAKIN'S BLUE LIGHTSABER	HAD AN ABSENT FATHER	MISSING A LIMB	WISE, OLD MENTOR	SHORT AND SASSY	DESTROYS A PLANET-KILLING TOOL	HAD "A BAD FEELING ABOUT THIS"	NATURAL PILOT	COCKY CHARM	
ANAKIN SKYWALKER												
BB-8							X					
C-3PO					X				X			
CHEWBACCA								X				
FINN				X			X					
HAN SOLO												
KYLO REN												
LEIA ORGANA		X							X			
LUKE SKYWALKER	X		X		X			X				
MAZ KANATA				X			X					
OBI-WAN KENOBI			X			X						
PADMÉ AMIDALA												
POE DAMERON		X							X	X	X	
R2-D2								X	X			
REY	X		X					X		X		
YODA												

172

These common traits, themes, and events help connect
an expanding story that spans generations.

DROID	ON THE RUN	SAVES DROID FROM SCAVENGERS	SEVERLY INJURED BY LIGHTSABER	FORCE SENSITIVE	ASKS SON TO REMOVE A MASK	FORCE SPIRIT	FREQUENTS CANTINAS	CAPTURED BY VILLAINS	ROYAL BLOOD	ROMANTIC RELATIONSHIP FAILS	
											ANAKIN SKYWALKER
●	●										**BB-8**
●								●			
	●						●	●			**CHEWBACCA**
			●								**FINN**
	●			●			●	●			**HAN SOLO**
			●	●							**KYLO REN**
				●				●	●		**LEIA ORGANA**
				●				●			**LUKE SKYWALKER**
			●			●					**MAZ KANATA**
●	●			●							**OBI-WAN KENOBI**
	●							●		●	**PADMÉ AMIDALA**
	●										**POE DAMERON**
●								●			
	●	●		●				●			**REY**
				●		●					**YODA**

TIME AND SPACE

8 HOURS	
7 HOURS	
6 HOURS	
5 HOURS	
4 HOURS	
3 HOURS	
2 HOURS	
1 HOUR	
40 MINUTES	
20 MINUTES	
0 MINUTES	

Star Wars: Episode I The Phantom Menace

Star Wars: Episode II Attack of the Clones

Star Wars: Episode III Revenge of the Sith

Star Wars: Episode IV A New Hope

Star Wars: Episode V The Empire Strikes Back

Star Wars: Episode VI Return of the Jedi

Star Wars: Episode VII The Force Awakens

Rogue One: A Star Wars Story

Star Wars: The Clone Wars

Star Wars: The Clone Wars Season 1

Star Wars: The Clone Wars Season 2

Star Wars: The Clone Wars Season 3

Star Wars: The Clone Wars Season 4

Star Wars: The Clone Wars Season 5

Star Wars: The Clone Wars Season 6: The Lost Missions

Star Wars Rebels Spark of Rebellion

Star Wars Rebels Web Shorts

Star Wars Rebels Season 1

Star Wars Rebels Season 2

Star Wars Rebels Season 3

Dark Disciple

Ahsoka

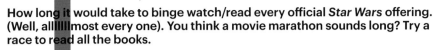

How long it would take to binge watch/read every official *Star Wars* offering. (Well, allllllmost every one). You think a movie marathon sounds long? Try a race to read all the books.

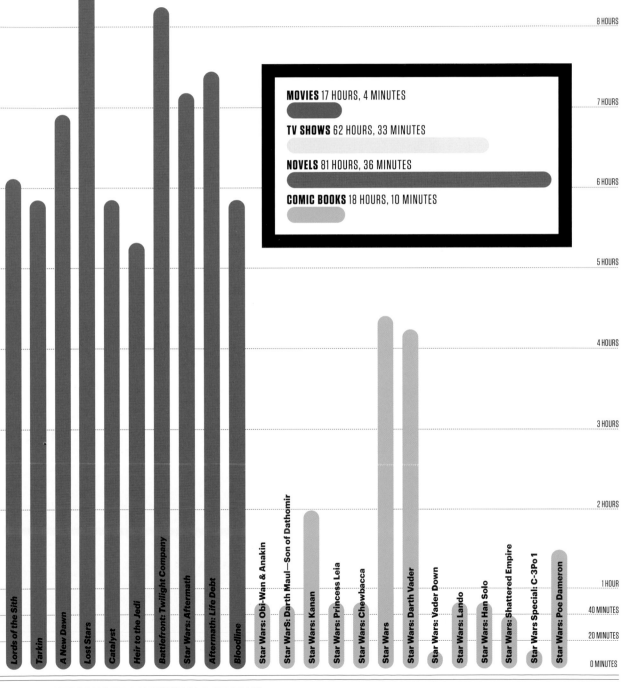

9 HOURS

8 HOURS

7 HOURS

6 HOURS

5 HOURS

4 HOURS

3 HOURS

2 HOURS

1 HOUR

40 MINUTES

20 MINUTES

0 MINUTES

MOVIES 17 HOURS, 4 MINUTES

TV SHOWS 62 HOURS, 33 MINUTES

NOVELS 81 HOURS, 36 MINUTES

COMIC BOOKS 18 HOURS, 10 MINUTES

Lords of the Sith

Tarkin

A New Dawn

Lost Stars

Catalyst

Heir to the Jedi

Battlefront: Twilight Company

Star Wars: Aftermath

Aftermath: Life Debt

Bloodline

Star Wars: Obi-Wan & Anakin

Star WarS: Darth Maul—Son of Dathomir

Star Wars: Kanan

Star Wars: Princess Leia

Star Wars: Chewbacca

Star Wars

Star Wars: Darth Vader

Star Wars: Vader Down

Star Wars: Lando

Star Wars: Han Solo

Star Wars: Shattered Empire

Star Wars Special: C-3Po 1

Star Wars: Poe Dameron

DOES NOT INCLUDE ALL YOUNG ADULT NOVELS OR SHORT STORIES

Tim Leong is the award-winning author of _Super Graphic: A Visual Guide to the Comic Book Universe_ (Best Art & Design Book of 2013, Amazon). He is also the Creative Director of _Entertainment Weekly_. His favorite Star Wars movie is _The Empire Strikes Back_, and he lives in Brooklyn with his Leia and their Jedi youngling.

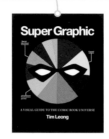

Library of Congress Cataloging-in-Publication Data is available.

ISBN 978-1-4521-6120-4

Manufactured in China

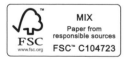

MIX
Paper from responsible sources
FSC™ C104723

10 9 8 7 6 5 4 3 2 1

Chronicle Books LLC
680 Second Street
San Francisco, California 94107
www.chroniclebooks.com

www.starwars.com

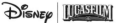

© & ™ 2017 LUCASFILM LTD.

WRITTEN AND DESIGNED BY

Tim Leong

ADDITIONAL DESIGN BY
Jennie Chang

ADDITIONAL ILLUSTRATIONS BY
James Kim

ADDITIONAL RESEARCH BY
Allie Sadlier

ADDITIONAL EDITING BY
Rachel Swaby

SPECIAL THANKS TO
Emily Haynes
Wynn Rankin
Neil Egan
Henry Goldblatt
Sean Smith
Keir Novesky
Caitlin Kennedy